MW01290424

Forever Paycheck

The Road to *Joyful* Retirement
with *Care-Free* Income

DEBBIE ANDREWS
KATHRYN PAYNE

Copyright © 2016 Andrews Financial Services

All rights reserved. No part of this publication may be used or reproduced, stored in a retrieval system, or transmitted, in any form or by any means, electronic, mechanical, photocopying, recording, or otherwise without the prior written permission of the publisher.

Investment Advisory Services are offered through Foundations Investment Advisors, LLC which is a SEC registered investment advisor.

ISBN-13: 978-1530628179

ISBN: 1530628172

Website: www.foreverpaycheck.com

Company location: Cypress Texas, USA

Cover designed by Jan Stephenson

DEDICATION

This book is dedicated to our families, friends, and clients.
We feel remarkably blessed to have you in our lives.

INTRODUCTION

Twenty years ago I met with Debbie Andrews to develop a financial plan. Today, I am 56 years old, retired and worry-free. I look back on that first day of planning, along with the many reviews and updates along the way, with much gratitude. I retired 6 years earlier than planned. And I have found the resulting gift of time, peace of mind, and the creative freedom that comes with it to be more valuable than I could have imagined.

Annuities are an important part of my investment portfolio. One reason I feel relaxed about my financial security is that I know I will have sufficient income to cover my needs for as long as I live – regardless of inevitable market swings. That said, annuities take some time to understand. The concepts are simple, but the language is unique. So, when Debbie proposed writing a book to help people understand how annuities fit into a long-term financial plan, I jumped at the opportunity to help.

Written in the voice of Debbie Andrews – a professional financial advisor – the book is designed to show you how to create a future paycheck that will work *for you* long after you stop working *for it*. How much will you need? How do you guarantee an income stream that will last for life? Will your current assumptions, beliefs, and investing behaviors produce the outcome you expect?

Debbie Andrews offers nearly 30 years of experience across multiple investment platforms. As co-author, I bring an investor's perspective. Our objective is to explain safe-money strategies, while keeping the financial jargon in check. If you are looking for facts, guidelines, and tools to help you develop a financial plan tailored for *your* unique situation, then look no further.

We believe that you will find this book to be informative and enjoyable. We wish you a lifetime of success – including a joyful and carefree retirement.

Kathryn Payne
Co-Author and Satisfied Retiree

AUTHOR'S NOTE TO READER

This book is *not* designed to provide personal investment advice of any kind. Each reader's unique circumstances and objectives must be considered when determining the most appropriate financial strategy. It's important to note that investment strategies are influenced by laws and commercially available financial instruments, which are subject to change. Consult with a professional financial advisor to discuss options in light of your personal objectives, financial situation, market conditions, current laws, and available financial products. Only pursue financial strategies which are in your own specific and personal best interest. The intent of this book is to introduce some of the distinctive benefits annuities can offer as part of a balanced financial portfolio. Always remember that your circumstances are unique. Consult with a professional before making any investment decision. There is simply no cookie-cutter approach for planning your future.

"An investment in knowledge pays the best interest."
Benjamin Franklin

Table of Contents

It's Not About Money 1

    What Do You Want From Your Retirement?.................. 2

    Plan for a Satisfying Retirement.................................... 4

    Funding your Funning 5

    Why do you invest?.. 6

    The Test of Time 6

    The Power of Annuities 9

Live Long and Prosper 11

    Living Longer Healthier Lives.................................... 11

    Retirement Income Has to Last Longer...................... 12

    Ladies Pay Attention!.. 13

    Take the Initiative... 13

    Three Steps to Freedom 14

Annuities: A Safe Money Strategy 17

    Growth 18

    Tax Deferral.. 19

    Optional Guarantees 20

    Future Income — Timing and Methods....................... 21

Insuring Your Income 22

Getting Started 24

Three Models for Growth 27

Fixed Annuities: A Safe Haven... 28

Variable Annuities: Market Growth with Market Risk............. 30

Indexed Annuity: Best of Both Worlds............................ 31

How to Produce Lifetime Income 35

Withdrawals 36

Income Riders... 39

Annuitization 59

Immediate Income... 65

Which option is best? 70

Are Annuity Companies Safe?... 73

Highly Regulated Industry 74

Industry Track Record 75

Doing Your Homework 75

Safety Strategies 76

Kiss the Dragons 79

You Can't Beat an Index 80

The Myth of Average Returns 90

When Buy and Hold Breaks Down.. 95

Inflation: The Income Eater 100

The Risk of Cognitive Decline 101

Misconceptions about Annuities 102

Is An Annuity Right For You? 117

What Is Your Number? 119

Income Replacement Rate 120

The 4 Percent Rule 123

Planning From the Bottom Up 126

Start Here 137

Supplement: Just for Fun! 139

About the Authors 143

Resources 145

"The authors make a very strong case for considering annuities in retirement planning by going beyond the dollars and sense, asking people to re-examine what they truly want retirement to be. This easy-to-read book enables a layperson to understand what annuities are and where they fit. An excellent read."

Dr. Jack Marrion
Founder of Safe Money Places and Advantage Compendium.

Dr. Marrion's research on senior decision making and the financial world have been featured in Business Week, Kiplinger, Smart Money, and The Wall Street Journal. He is the author of six books and a frequent media guest.

1

It's Not About Money

"Many people take no care of their money till they come to the end of it, and others do just the same with their time." Johann Wolfgang von Goethe

It may sound odd to start a book about income with a statement like "it's not about money," but it's important to remember that money is not the *reason* we save. It's merely an enabler. It's not the car, it's the oil. A quart of oil without a car to put it in is boring.

During our earning years, we dream of retirement, sacrificing some of our present-day to fund our future. Our imaginations play with the options like children play with toys — picturing endless possibilities. Fun with family and friends. A home with a view. Time for hobbies. Travel. New skills and interests. And that is exactly what retirement should be. *Fun!*

What Do You Want From Your Retirement?

I recently came across an article titled "20 Things We Do in Retirement[1]." I eagerly snapped it up, trolling for tips on how to create a fun and rewarding retirement. You can imagine my surprise when I read the conclusion: "You'll spend your time watching TV and puttering around the house." What? No! I don't know about you, but that's not what I was picturing.

On one hand, labor economists and study authors Charlene Kalenkoski and Eakamon Oumtrakool make a refreshing observation — retirement can be affordable. They rightly point out that spending time at home relaxing, thinking, reading, and watching TV doesn't cost a lot of money[2]. True. We'll discuss how the costs of future activities can impact retirement planning in the last chapter. Perhaps you will even conclude that you don't need a zillion dollars to retire happily, despite what the investment media might proclaim. Thinking through post-retirement expenses, recognizing how spending patterns inevitably shift, is a helpful exercise.

On the other hand, the study's findings are a serious wake-up call. Think about it. Most of us will spend nearly a third of our life in retirement, and we expect this time to be fulfilling. While spending some time couch-surfing and relaxing may sound appealing in the short run, it's not enough to maintain an active and healthy mind in the long run. Watching too many reruns of *Six Feet Under* will likely accelerate the process. The worst thing retirees can do after decades of busy, stimulating work is to stop challenging their brains with new interests and experiences.

Research shows that retirees who are involved in diverse mental and physical activities are the most likely to thrive. In a recent study[3], the Sloan Center on Aging and Work at Boston College found that an overall sense of well-being can be linked directly to a higher level of engagement. Older adults who actively participate in work, volunteering, care-giving, or educational activities report significantly higher levels of life satisfaction and mental health than more idle peers. So, when planning for fulfillment during the leisure years, set your mind on changing paths, not speed.

Terri Bieber, Director of Creative Aging at Mamie George Community Center[4], specializes in the connection between good health and creative endeavors. According to Bieber, the people who age best are the ones who find a variety of ways to stay active. "They learn new skills, dabble in the arts, take classes and go to lectures, stay engaged with family members, and develop new friendships and social networks." Her mantra? "Don't just stay busy — stay creative!"

"It's not enough to be busy; so are the ants. The question is: What are we busy about?" Henry David Thoreau

If you don't plan for an active and interesting retirement, the chances that you'll create one later are slim. Many people assume that it will be easy to find interesting activities in retirement, so they barely give it a second thought. Don't be so sure. The top five retiree activities in Kalenkoski and Oumtrakool's study were sleeping, watching TV and movies, eating and drinking, reading, and grooming. Yawn.

It doesn't have to be that way though. History books are filled with people who did their best and most creative work in their later years. Picasso produced a flood of paintings and etchings when he was pushing 90, becoming even more daring, colorful, and expressive in his later years. Michelangelo designed St. Peter's cupola at 83. Ronald Reagan served two terms in the White House after age 65. At 80 years old, Verdi wrote Falstaff, the last of his 28 operas. Nelson Mandela became president of South Africa at 76. Georgia O'Keeffe started working with clay, pencil, and charcoal in her 80's and 90's when her eyesight was severely compromised.

Big accomplishments are possible when you "retire." So, forget the rocking chair and plan big! Seize the time and freedom that retirement can offer and channel it for your own brand of creative, intellectual, physical, social, and philanthropic enjoyment. Go for it!

Plan for a Satisfying Retirement

We're going to get to your finances in a minute, but start by thinking about what you want from your retirement. No satisfaction will come from simply staking your claim on a mountain of cash when you land on retirement's shores. Had Columbus planted his flag on new soil and gone home without exploring, trading, and building – history might have passed him by.

Reclaim from the back burner every wild idea, wistful fantasy and personal indulgence you ever entertained. Make your ideas alive with details and extensions! If travel is on your list, enhance the list with your top ten (or more) destinations. Thinking about traveling to France? Maybe you would like to live there instead.

Mix and match ideas for double enjoyment. Love gardening? Activate your inner entrepreneur and start a container gardening business. Are you an aspiring artist? Check out local options for renting studio space and share the space with a fellow artist for some social stimulation. Sign up for one of Road Scholar's art retreats and quench your travel thirst at the same time. Have you always wanted to know more about (fill in the blank)? Take a class. Join a study group or create one if it doesn't exist. Or find out if your local university will allow you to audit a class for free.

This line of thinking is not intended to lead you through a complete planning process for retirement fun. It is simply meant to acknowledge that planning how you will invest retirement years for maximum enjoyment and development is just as important as planning for the income to support it. Time is a gift. Money might help you enjoy it, but it won't tell you how to get the most from it.

Funding your Funning

"Money does not make you happy but it quiets the nerves." Sean O'Casey, Playwright, 1880-1964

While stimulation is clearly important, you can't deny the fact that you'll need some money. That means you'll need a plan for funding all of that funning. Having enough money to cover your basic needs plus a few perks in retirement – however long you may live – is **peace of mind worth its weight in gold.**

Babe Ruth, Ben Bernanke, Caesar, Beethoven, Benjamin Franklin, and Andrew Carnegie can offer pointers about that kind of freedom. Do you know what they hold in common? All of them created paths to future income — paychecks that would last long beyond the working years – secured through a simple financial vehicle called an annuity.

Now, before you hit the auto-eject button based on some vague preconception you may have about what annuities can and can't do, let's peel the onion a few layers – starting with a fundamental question: Why do you invest?

Why do you invest?

Think deeply about this question. Ask stock market enthusiasts what motivates them to invest in stocks, and you are likely to hear words like **wealth, rate of return, and growth**. Mutual fund investors will emphasize **diversification, reduced risk and convenience** – freely admitting that they don't have the time or inclination to research stocks, monitor the market and allocate assets. Real estate investors generally favor the idea of **cash flow** and **appreciation**. Ask this question frequently enough and the list of reasons will start to repeat.

After nearly 30 years as a financial advisor, I am baffled by how rarely I hear what I consider to be *the most important objective*:

Future income! You need a paycheck that will work *for you* long after you stop working *for it*. And **annuities are one of the strongest ways to get it.**

The Test of Time

Although annuities today have a lot of bells and whistles suited for our contemporary world, the idea is not new.

Caesar Knew How to Reward His Soldiers

Annuities date back to the Roman times when Caesar provided a lifetime income to soldiers and their families as a thank you for their military service[5]. In fact, the word annuity comes from the Latin word "Annua" which means annual payment or stipend. Can you imagine the loyalty Caesar engendered by securing a financial future for soldiers and their families? I doubt there were many professions at the time that could offer such a compelling deal.

Beethoven Got an Offer He Couldn't Refuse

When King Jerome Bonaparte, offered Ludwig van Beethoven a lucrative position to move back to Germany in 1809, Viennese dignitaries intervened and offered him a generous annuity. The only requirement was that he remain in Vienna to pursue his passion for composing and performing. Beethoven seized the opportunity to have a lifetime income, and Austria won the battle for talent. Many of Beethoven's most admired works came from the last 15 years of his life when he had the freedom to create[6].

Andrew Carnegie: Oil Baron, Philanthropist and Pension King

Andrew Carnegie was known as a steel baron and philanthropist, but you might not know that he was seminal figure in pension fund history. A pension is an annuity. It offers income for life, and Carnegie knew the value of that. His initial funding launched what became the U.S. Steel & Carnegie Pension Fund and the Teacher's Insurance Annuity Association (TIAA). Teachers still benefit from these annuity offerings through the same company now known as TIAA-CREF[7]. These are thriving examples of how annuities were used then and still today to secure the financial future for thousands of aging workers.

Two Cities Reap the Benefits of Benjamin Franklin's Annuities

In 1785, Benjamin Franklin left each of the cities of Boston and Philadelphia £1,000 in trust (about $125,000 in today's dollars) to gather interest for 200 years. By 1990, the two trust funds contained more than $7,000,000. The cities used the money to support a variety of services – establishing a trade school (Franklin Institute of Boston), offering loans to residents, and providing scholarships for local high school students[8]. Want to understand the benefits of an annuity? Ask Philadelphia and Boston.

Babe Ruth Lives Comfortably Through the Great Depression

Babe Ruth put his World Series winnings and portions of his salary into annuities between the years 1923-1929. In 1935, he was forced to retire from baseball as his physical abilities waned – in the *heart of the Great Depression*! His financial plan paid off though, and he began receiving annuity payments of $17,500 per year (equivalent to $290,578 in today's dollars). During an era of deep financial turmoil, Babe and his wife were able to live comfortably in retirement without fear of running out of money. He was so impressed with the financial freedom afforded by the power of annuities that he directed his estate to purchase a lifetime income annuity for his wife after his death[9].

Former Fed Chief Ben Bernanke Ought to Know

Flash forward to the 21st century, and you'll find that annuities are still favored by some of the world's most influential leaders. In fact, former Federal Reserve Chairman Ben Bernanke's largest investment holdings are annuities — one fixed and one variable — according to annual government reports[10]. When it comes to financial security, one could argue that a Federal Reserve Chairman would be a decent role model.

A Legal Guard

While you might not appreciate this particular example, OJ Simpson's annuity protected his income from lawsuits and creditors[11]. I hope you never need protection from lawsuits or creditors, but sometimes the unexpected occurs. And if it does, it's nice to know that annuities can offer this kind of shield for future income. (Note: Laws regarding these legal protections vary by state.)

Even Uncle Sam Likes Annuities

In 2014, the U.S. Department of the Treasury issued guidance encouraging the use of income annuities in 401(k) plans and IRAs in order to boost lifetime income and retirement security[12]. The IRS and Department of Labor agree with the Treasury on this advice. In fact, the U.S. Government Accountability Office advises middle-class retirees to convert at least half of their retirement savings into an annuity[13].

The Power of Annuities

My objective is to awaken you to the power of annuities to create your financial freedom. Annuities are the only financial instrument available today that can offer you:

- Guaranteed protection of your principal and gains.
- Tax deferred growth.
- Guaranteed income for life.
- Control over when your income is distributed.

When it comes to security for both growth and future income, no one has a crystal ball. Babe Ruth did not know that the roaring 20's would dissolve into the Great Depression when he purchased his first annuities. Yet, when the market made an unexpected turn precisely in the moment Babe needed his money the most, his annuities delivered as promised.

2

Live Long and Prosper

"Old age is the most unexpected of all things that happen to a man."
Leon Trotsky

We all hope to follow Spock's guidance to "live long and prosper," yet predicting how many years we might have to support ourselves is one of the most mystifying hurdles we face in saving for our future.

Living Longer Healthier Lives

The good news is that we're living longer. Thanks to advances in science and technology, life expectancies have more than doubled in the past century. Recent Centers for Disease Control and Prevention (CDC) studies showed the average life expectancy in the U.S. to be 78.8 years in 2012, up from 78.7 in 2011. This is the longest life expectancy ever recorded[14]. Since the death rates of children and young adults are very low in the U.S., additional increases in life expectancy come from further improvements in the oldest age groups. The CDC attributes the longevity increase to a reduction in many major causes of death, such as cancer, heart disease, and stroke.

In wealthy nations, the mortality rate for people older than 80 years continues to decline. According to data from more than thirty developed countries, in 1950 the probability of survival from age 80 to 90 years averaged 15 to 16 percent for women and 12 percent for men. In 2002, these values were 37 percent and 25 percent. If current life expectancy trends continue, **more than half of babies born in wealthy nations today will live to 100 years.**[15]

Retirement Income Has to Last Longer

Not only are we living longer, we are adding healthy years with less disability and fewer limitations than in the past. That's great news, yet it means that our retirement income has to last longer than we may think.

Data from Statistic Brain Research Institute show that the average person today will retire at 63 and spend 18 years in retirement. Of course, *your* retirement could easily last longer than today's average. The National Institute on Aging projects that **the 85-and-over population will increase 351 percent** between 2010 and 2050[16], and **the number of centenarians will soar tenfold**[17]. Actuaries estimate that about 25% of couples who are healthy at 65 will have at least one spouse live longer than 97 years.

~ Could you support yourself for 20-30 years or more? ~

Ladies Pay Attention!

"Nothing is more dangerous to men [or women] than a sudden change of fortune." Quintilian

Almost half the women over 65 years of age in the United States are widows. About 7 in 10 of these women live alone (U.S. Census, 2000). According to the U.S. Census Bureau, nearly 700,000 women lose their husbands each year and will be widows for an average of 14 years[18]. In recent years, the average American woman's expected lifespan has increased to eighty or more. **Every woman needs a plan for supporting herself now and into the future.**

Take the Initiative

Eighty percent of people ages 30-54 do not think that they will have enough money put away for retirement. **Luckily people in this age range generally have the time and resources to *do something about it*!** The average 50-year old only has $42,797 in savings. Out of 100 people who start working at the age of 25, only 4% will have adequate capital stowed away for retirement by the age 65. Sixty-three percent will be dependent on Social Security, friends, relatives or charity to meet their needs[19].

Can you imagine the stress that must accompany the sudden realization that you may not have enough monthly income to cover your basic needs? Or that you could run out of money before you run out of life?

~ Why isn't future income at the top of everyone's list of goals? ~

Income we can count on is our most basic need. If we want to maintain our standard of living after we retire, we need to plan to afford the goods and services we rely upon, whether we live to 80,

90, 100, or longer.

Three Steps to Freedom

"Money equals freedom." Kevin O'Leary

This book is about **freedom**. By the end, you will know how to **create your forever paycheck.** The goal is to ensure that you **never worry about how you will pay your bills** or whether your money will run dry. The aim is to **meet your day to day needs in retirement** while allowing you to **enjoy the finer things in life:** family, friends, travel, giving ... whatever activities bring you the most joy.

This book is about **peace of mind.** I don't know about you, but for my own peace of mind, I insure everything I can — my house, my car, my health, my life, my household goods, and jewelry. I want to know that I can recover if my house burns to the ground, my car is wrecked, my health takes a hit, or a thief pilfers the goods. If I were to tell you that you could **insure your future income** and protect it from loss, *while* benefiting from market growth, wouldn't your ears perk up?

In fact, you can! **You can benefit from market upside, avoid the downside, and create your own forever paycheck.** Too good to be true? No. The financial vehicle — an Indexed Annuity — exists today. This is one of three different kinds of annuities that I'll explain later.

With this book, I would like to help you crystallize your retirement objectives while giving you the real story on annuities — what they are, how they work, where they fit, pros and cons. Then you will be armed with the information you need to decide for yourself whether annuities are a good fit for your specific requirements and financial future.

The following chapters will lead you through three steps to retirement freedom.

- **Step 1: Understand your options.** We'll start with the basics. You can't make informed decisions without a clear understanding of what's available to you. This chapter provides a simple overview of the general types of annuities on the market today, describes how they work, and offers perspectives on why and when they make sense — from a layman's perspective. My goal is to keep the financial jargon in check and to boil annuities down to their essence.

- **Step 2: Challenge your investment assumptions with a laser focus on your objective — sustainable income for life.** Sometimes our beliefs and behaviors get in the way. I will walk you through common misconceptions and market assumptions that could falsely shape your decision-making process, point out how misconceptions can trip you up, and provide sample strategies to ensure the traps don't stand between you and your forever paycheck.

- **Step 3: Develop a blueprint for lifetime income**. You wouldn't build a quality house without a blueprint. And you shouldn't build your financial future without a blueprint either. The final chapter will cover processes for planning your retirement nest egg – helping you think through how much money you will need. You will find some pointers on post-retirement expenses, including research on how spending patterns typically shift. Eventually, you'll want to engage a financial advisor skilled in retirement strategies to support your unique requirements and planning process, but this should get you started.

Since nothing speaks louder than numbers when exploring investment concepts, I will frequently use a fictitious investor who I'll call Joe Investor to illustrate portfolio performance under various circumstances. In most examples, we'll imagine that Joe has a nest egg of $500,000 by the time he's ready to retire. As you know by now, this is statistically more than many people have when they approach retirement. It is also far less than most middle class investors will actually want for a worry-free retirement.

To keep the examples consistent and easy to follow, I will generally use one snapshot in time – a 20-year period from 1990 to 2010. I selected this timeframe for two reasons: (1) there are several studies and statistical references which make it interesting, and (2) the up and down patterns of the market during this period are classic and instructive. Naturally, different market snapshots will yield unique results. I encourage you to plug in your own assumptions when evaluating options that make sense for you.

I have also included examples from real life. In these cases, I used actual situations, but changed the investor's names and unique details to protect their privacy.

The purpose of this book is to help you plan ahead for *your* forever paycheck. The examples can work whether you have $100,000 or $100 million. The math is the same. But, keep in mind that what *you* need will be entirely different from what your neighbor may need. Consult a financial advisor before you make investment decisions. Your circumstances are unique, and there is simply no cookie-cutter approach for planning your future.

3

Annuities: A Safe Money Strategy

"Put your trust not in money, put your money in trust." Sir Oliver Wendell Holmes

Strip away all of the fancy financial lingo, and you'll find that annuities aren't that complicated. **An annuity is a long term investment with tax advantages supported by** *optional* **guarantees**.

At the highest level, they are defined by four basic characteristics:

1. Growth
2. Tax deferral
3. Optional guarantees
4. Future income

Figure 1

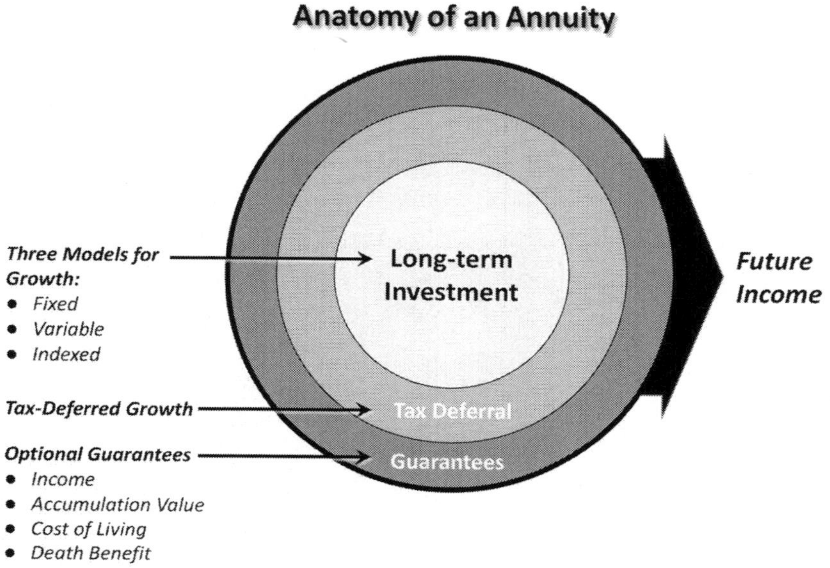

Anatomy of an Annuity

Three Models for Growth:
- Fixed
- Variable
- Indexed

Long-term Investment

Future Income

Tax-Deferred Growth → Tax Deferral

Optional Guarantees → Guarantees
- Income
- Accumulation Value
- Cost of Living
- Death Benefit

Growth

At the heart of every annuity lies a simple investment. Similar to other investments you may have made in your past, various growth models are available and you will want to select a model that suits your financial objectives and risk tolerance.

Annuities offer three different flavors of growth:

- **Fixed** annuities are interest based. They offer a predetermined rate of return for a set period of time and are generally considered to be a safe haven.
- **Variable** annuities are market-based in that they are invested in securities such as stocks, bonds, money markets and related assets. Variable annuities have *unit values* that

rise and fall according to the performance of the underlying investments, called "sub-accounts."

- **Indexed** are a type of fixed annuity which *follow* the performance of a particular market index such as the S&P 500, Dow Jones Industrial Average or NASDAQ. They provide downside protection from market volatility, offering a nice blend of growth and safety.

Tax Deferral

All annuities provide **tax-deferred growth**, meaning that you do not pay taxes on your *gains* until the money is withdrawn in the future. Tax-deferred growth is a **standard benefit provided by all annuities**.

There are **two possibilities when it comes to taxing your** *principal* (i.e., your initial deposit or premium). When you make your deposit, you will decide whether to use pre-tax or post-tax money. If you have ever made the choice to invest in an IRA or 401k, then this is a concept you will recognize.

- **Qualified annuities** use pre-tax money "qualified" for IRS income tax deferral. Financial vehicles like Individual Retirement Accounts (IRA), Simplified Employee Pension (SEP), and 401k accounts contain qualified funds. The money in these types of accounts may be invested in annuities. You pay income taxes on this principal when you withdraw the money. Uncle Sam tells us how much of today's money we can sock away for tomorrow's taxes, so the amount of new pre-tax funds you can put into your annuity each year will be directed by law. Required minimum distributions for qualified funds must start no later than age 70 ½. If you currently have funds in a 401k, SEP or IRA, and you wish to roll this into an annuity – this can be a simple procedure. Talk to your advisor to understand if and how it may apply to your particular contract.

- **Non-qualified annuities** use post-tax money (i.e., money for which you have already paid your income taxes). "Non-qualified" simply means that your initial deposit is "not qualified" for tax deduction in the current year. Post-tax deposits will benefit from **tax-deferred** *growth*. You will pay taxes only on the gains when you withdraw the money. Non-qualified annuities do not have required distributions at 70 ½. This offers the owner more flexibility in deciding when distributions make sense given their personal situation.

Because annuities offer tax advantages, the IRS imposes rules regarding withdrawal. Like an IRA or 401k, the IRS will charge a penalty if you withdraw money before you are 59 1/2 years old. Annuities, therefore, are considered to be retirement savings vehicles by nature.

Optional Guarantees

Bankers or stock brokers can offer you other financial vehicles for fixed, variable or indexed growth, and even put your money in a tax deferred package like an IRA — but they cannot offer lifetime guarantees. **A guarantee is** *insurance* —only offered by insurance companies, in an industry regulated for your safety. So, think of an annuity's optional guarantees as **insurance that can be "bolted onto" your central investment** to help you meet your financial objectives.

The insurance company offers various **insurance benefits** that *ride on top of your annuity* – called "**riders**," of course. Depending on the type of annuity you select, either by design or through riders, annuities offer you the opportunity to:

- Insure your future income – an enticing offering given the topic of this book.
- Adjust your future income streams to help with cost of living increases.
- Provide a death benefit for your heirs.

Options can be mixed and matched according to your objectives and the type of investment you select. For example, a volatile variable annuity would benefit from a guaranteed minimum accumulation value rider, whereas an indexed annuity wouldn't need it. The downside protection built into the indexed contracts already provides a guarantee — a benefit which will be explained in more detail shortly. Your financial advisor will be able to describe the options and help you select the riders that might make sense for you.

For the purposes of this book, we are assuming that reliable future income is one of your key objectives, so **annuities — with the income guarantees they can offer — are uniquely qualified**.

Future Income — Timing and Methods

One of the questions your advisor may ask when you purchase your annuity is whether you need income now or later.

- **Deferred** annuities mean that you will delay taking money from your account until some specified time in the future. A deferred annuity has an accumulation period allowing your money to grow between your initial deposit and the beginning of your income stream years later.

- **Immediate** annuities mean that you want income right away. An immediate annuity has no accumulation period and generally requires a fixed growth model.

Income distribution happens when you initiate a forever paycheck from your annuity. Usually, you will begin to distribute funds at age 59 ½ or older. This is the age when Uncle Sam allows you to access tax deferred money without penalty.

There are **two options for getting your money** out of an annuity: withdrawals or guaranteed income streams.

- **Withdrawals** can be random or systematic, and you may choose the amount and frequency *without initiating guaranteed income*. At the end of your term, you generally have easy access to your funds without restrictions. If you need money before your term is up, most annuities allow you to withdraw a certain amount per year without contractual penalties. Remember, however, that the IRS will still charge taxes plus penalties on interest earned for withdrawals before age 59 ½.
- **A guaranteed income stream** is an option unique to annuities. There are two ways to arrange this forever paycheck: **(1) An income rider** provides options regarding the distribution of your forever paycheck while allowing access to your cash accumulation account. **(2) Annuitization** is an *irrevocable* process of converting an annuity into a forever paycheck which cannot be changed once enacted.

Insuring Your Income

"I may take risks in life, but I will never risk my money. I use annuities and I never have to worry about my money." Babe Ruth

When you purchase car insurance or home insurance, you are making a decision to cover the risk of potential losses. When you buy an annuity, you are doing the same thing. In this case, you are covering the risk that your money will run out before you die. In other words, **annuities insure your retirement income.** At their core, annuities are *insurance* products offered by life insurance companies. If you start by understanding this basic fact, then it will be easier to understand the opportunities, limitations and language of annuities.

Because of their unique ability to insure your **income as long as you live**, annuities are considered to be one of the most **powerful tools for retirement planning**. It's important to realize that replacing income later in life may be unrealistic or even impossible, so retirees who run out of money could be in a difficult jam when it comes to supporting themselves. Annuities are designed to keep you out of this jam.

~ Annuities are like life insurance in reverse ~

Conceptually speaking, annuities are like life insurance in reverse. Life insurance pays someone else upon your death, while annuities pay *you* while you're living.

When you buy an annuity, you agree to deposit your money (called a premium) for a period of time. In return, the insurance company provides growth and offers various guarantees. While you are **benefiting from tax deferred growth and optional income guarantees**, the insurance company (like a bank or any other financial institution) is assuming that it can earn more over time than it will have to pay you.

When and *if* you elect to activate income guarantees, these contracts are **guaranteed to pay out** on a periodic basis until your death, **even if the total payments exceed the amount you put into the contract** plus any accrued interest or gain. This option of turning your investment into a guaranteed income stream is **unique to annuities**. In this book, we will often call that guaranteed income stream your "forever paycheck" – because it is future income that you simply won't have to worry about.

~ Lingo Alert ~
Premium = Deposit = Principal = *Your money*

Life insurance companies call your deposit into an annuity a "premium." Many clients find this term to be confusing, and I understand why. We are used to paying a premium for car and home insurance, so we tend to think of it as a sunk cost that the insurance company keeps unless there's an accident. Right? Not so with annuities. Your premium is your deposit and principal. It is still your money. It will grow inside the annuity and you will withdraw it, along with gains, at the end of your term – or you will turn it into an income stream. So, don't be confused or worried by this insurance lingo. In the case of annuities, a premium is simply a deposit.

Getting Started

To recap, when you purchase an annuity, these are the four key decisions you will need to make.

- Which kind of growth profile aligns best with your objectives and risk tolerance? Fixed, variable, or indexed?
- When do you need your money? Immediately or later?
- What funds will you put into the annuity? Pre-tax (qualified) and/or post-tax (non-qualified) funds?
- What kinds of guarantees are important to you? Income, accumulation, cost of living, death benefits?

As you would with any other important investment, you should consult a financial professional to help you choose a model appropriate for your personal circumstances and objectives. In this case, find an advisor who is licensed and experienced in the field of annuities. To sell an annuity, the financial advisor must have a license to sell insurance. To sell variable annuities, the advisor must be licensed to sell both insurance and securities.

4

Three Models for Growth

"A simple fact that is hard to learn is that the time to save money is when you have some." Joe Moore

All annuities allow tax-deferred growth and provide options for guaranteed lifetime income.

In addition, because annuities are insurance products, they offer another subtle and valuable benefit. You are able to specify **beneficiaries** to receive your money upon your death. Your heirs will appreciate this feature, because it means they will get the funds immediately, **without the headache, heartache and delay of probate court**. (NOTE: A few states do not allow bypass of probate. Check with your financial advisor to validate the rules in your state.)

Annuities begin to take different shapes when it comes to the growth model applied to your initial investment. You will choose between three basic growth structures – fixed, variable, or indexed – selecting the one that matches your financial goals and risk tolerance. If safety is of primary importance to you, you may choose the guaranteed rates of return offered by fixed annuities. If you can tolerate the downside risk for the chance of higher returns, variable annuities might be your cup of tea. If you want some of both — market-based growth with downside protection — then indexed annuities would fill the bill.

Fixed Annuities: A Safe Haven

A fixed annuity pays a **fixed rate of return for a specific period of time** and would be considered to be a **safe investment**. It is similar to a Certificate of Deposit (CD) in this respect – with the added feature of tax deferral. As is true for most safe investments, the interest rates on fixed annuities are relatively low compared to other investments, so the potential for growth is limited.

During an agreed period of time, funds in fixed annuities are less accessible than bank account funds in that they charge penalties for early withdrawals. This kind of accessibility is analogous to the treatment you would experience with a CD. Financial institutions can afford to offer you higher interest rates because they have some assurance that you'll stick with the plan, and leave your money with them for a while.

That's where the similarities between a CD and Fixed Annuity end, however. Even at exactly the same interest rate, a Fixed Annuity will top CD performance on multiple fronts: tax-deferred growth, beneficiaries, and income.

As shown in Figure 2, growth on fixed annuities is better than CDs because of tax treatment. Fixed annuity growth is tax-deferred (meaning that you pay taxes on the gains later, when you withdraw the money), whereas the gains on a CD are taxed every year. That extra money compounds in the fixed annuity over time, super-charging the return. Because the individual earns interest on the deferred amount – in addition to earning interest on the original principal and gains –the fixed annuity grows faster than a CD paying the same interest rate.

Figure 2

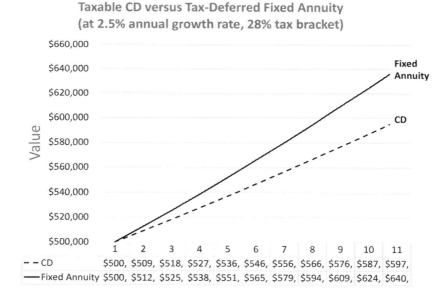

Taxable CD versus Tax-Deferred Fixed Annuity
(at 2.5% annual growth rate, 28% tax bracket)

	1	2	3	4	5	6	7	8	9	10	11
– – CD	$500,	$509,	$518,	$527,	$536,	$546,	$556,	$566,	$576,	$587,	$597,
Fixed Annuity	$500,	$512,	$525,	$538,	$551,	$565,	$579,	$594,	$609,	$624,	$640,

A fixed annuity will clearly outshine the return offered by a CD and, it will beat a bank savings account by a long shot. Because of this, many investors consider fixed annuities instead of bonds as their source of safe money.

As a reminder — fixed annuities are insurance products, so you can name your beneficiaries. In most states, your named **beneficiaries** can bypass probate court and receive the balance of your account immediately upon your death.

While these benefits alone are compelling, the **primary reason** a fixed annuity will trounce a CD and other "safe money" solutions (e.g., bonds) is **income!** Annuities offer a benefit that other financial vehicles simply can't provide – an option for **guaranteed income for life** – **peace of mind** from knowing that you will not outlive your money. This feature is unique to annuities.

Variable Annuities: Market Growth with Market Risk

Like fixed annuities, variable annuities allow tax-deferred growth, an option for guaranteed lifetime income and, in most states allow beneficiaries to bypass probate.

The **key difference between variable annuities and the other two types of annuities is risk**. Similar to a mutual fund, the growth of a variable annuity is based primarily on securities such as stocks, bonds, money market instruments and related assets. When the underlying investments benefit from a market up-cycle, the variable annuity value grows. In a down-cycle, the value declines. Variable annuities can win or lose depending on the volatility of the market. Unlike fixed and indexed annuities which won't lose money, the value of variable annuities can fall below your initial deposit in a weak market. You must shoulder the risk of market declines in exchange for the possibility that the opposite will happen, allowing you to earn a higher return.

Similar to mutual funds, variable annuities come with management fees and various other charges that fixed annuities do not. When viewed through the lens of lifetime income, you will have to decide whether the extra risk and cost are justified by the opportunity for higher returns. There are many investors who believe in the risk-reward formula offered by variable annuities.

Discuss the alternatives with a qualified financial advisor so that your particular circumstances and interests may be considered. Be sure to ask about all fees and costs associated with your contract – whether it's an annuity or any other investment. We'll discuss specific fee structures in a later chapter.

Indexed Annuity: Best of Both Worlds

"Rule #1: Never lose money. Rule #2: Never forget rule #1." Warren Buffett

If the mild returns of a fixed annuity make you yawn, and the risks of a variable annuity make you twitch, then an indexed annuity might be just what the doctor ordered. It offers an ideal balance of safety and growth. Here's how:

The indexed annuity provides safety by: (1) protecting your principal and interest earned and (2) insulating your investment from stock market declines.

Growth is tied to a market index such as the S&P 500, Dow Jones Industrial Average, or NASDAQ — so **if the market goes up you get to keep a certain percentage of that gain** – generally bound by a cap. For example, if your cap is 5%, and the market rises 10%, then you would receive a 5% credit to your base account value. If the market goes up 0-5%, then you keep the full amount. The cap simply defines how much of the market gain you get to keep. On the flip side, if the market has a negative return – even if it's one of those gut-wrenching 30-50% declines – you won't lose a penny.

Gains without losses: Think about how valuable that is over time. If you want to see the math, take a look at the examples in the next chapter ("Kiss the Dragons, The Myth of Average Returns").

An indexed annuity offers another even more significant benefit. **The base value of the indexed annuity** *resets* **as the market rises.** Every year, the **gains you realized are locked in** so that the higher value becomes your new floor. In other words, not only is your principal protected, your growth is protected too. For example, if you put in $100,000 and earn 5%, your new base account value (or basis) will be $105,000. You can never lose that extra $5,000 gain.

Regarding value year to year, there are only two options with an indexed annuity. Either the value goes up with the market. Or it stays flat, because the market declined. Figure 3 shows what would have happened to $100,000 in a market like we experienced between the years 2000 and 2010 had that money been invested (a) directly in the S&P 500 market[20] subject to normal market swings — assuming that the average investor actually could have earned these percentages (more on this improbability later), or (b) in an indexed annuity with downside protection and a 5% cap.

In the market example on the left, it took our imaginary investor over *six years* simply to break even after suffering from three years of market losses. In ten years, he only made $4,003 on his original investment (less than 0.4% per year). Yikes! Meanwhile, our indexed annuity investor on the right was protected from the losses during the bad years, allowing him to benefit from the gains immediately when the market turned the corner. He earned $40,428.62 in the same time frame, *in the same market*. Even with a 5% cap on the gains, the sample indexed annuity outperformed the pure market by an impressive margin because of the downside protection. Plus, each time the market increased, the gain was locked into the investor's base account value (basis).

Figure 3: Market Versus Indexed Annuity

Year	A) Invested in the Market*		B) Indexed Annuity with downside protection with 5% growth cap	
	Return	Account Value	Return	Account Value
Starting Point		$ 100,000.00		$ 100,000.00
2000	-9.11%	$ 90,890.00	0.00%	$ 100,000.00
2001	-11.98%	$ 80,001.38	0.00%	$ 100,000.00
2002	-22.27%	$ 62,185.07	0.00%	$ 100,000.00
2003	28.72%	$ 80,044.62	5.00%	$ 105,000.00
2004	10.82%	$ 88,705.45	5.00%	$ 110,250.00
2005	4.79%	$ 92,954.44	4.79%	$ 115,530.98
2006	15.74%	$ 107,585.47	5.00%	$ 121,307.52
2007	5.46%	$ 113,459.64	5.00%	$ 127,372.90
2008	-37.22%	$ 71,229.96	0.00%	$ 127,372.90
2009	27.11%	$ 90,540.40	5.00%	$ 133,741.54
2010	14.87%	$ 104,003.76	5.00%	$ 140,428.62

*Source of returns: MoneyChimp.com
Illustration does not include trading costs or fees.

If you need a spine-chilling demonstration, then check out 2008, when the S&P 500 tanked! Look what happened in the prior example. Indexed annuity owners didn't lose a cent. Not only were they insulated from the market decline, their previous gains were protected as well. When the market turned the corner and started to climb, the money in indexed annuities followed it up, making new gains from previously locked-in highs. Meanwhile, other account owners scrambled to get back to their starting point.

Naturally, the numbers will vary depending on market performance, specific annuity offerings and contractual terms. However, it's **hard to argue with the kind of value that comes from downside protection.**

Like all annuities, the indexed annuity shares the common thread: tax-deferred growth, bypass of probate (in most states), and the option for a guaranteed lifetime income. What's unique about an indexed annuity is that it provides market-style growth, within predefined bounds, while protecting your investment from stock market declines. **The value of your annuity can never be damaged by market volatility**.

Now, stop for moment and *really* **reflect on this**. Where else can you find a financial product with returns that track the upside potential of the market, with 100% downside protection, and locked-in gains? I have been a financial advisor for nearly three decades, and I haven't found anything close to an indexed annuity for maximizing future income. If you want lifetime income for a worry-free retirement, an indexed annuity is a unique and powerful tool.

5

How to Produce Lifetime Income

"When I was young I thought that money was the most important thing in life; now that I am old I know that it is." Oscar Wilde

Many investors, and even some financial advisors, have the **misconception that annuities lock up your money** forever or that you have to relinquish control of your funds to the insurance company. I would like to bust that myth forever!

With annuities you can:

- Enjoy returns equal to or greater than many other investments — with fixed, variable, and indexed options for growth.
- Super-charge your growth with **tax-deferred gains**.
- Maintain **control** of and **access** to your funds.
- Choose how you would like to manage your **future income** stream — ranging from random withdrawals (like any other

account) to guaranteed lifetime income streams (unique to annuities).

Annuities provide features similar to other conservative investments with one extra and significant benefit. Annuities provide the opportunity to convert your money into a **guaranteed paycheck for life**. This *optional* **feature** is **unique to annuities**. Because annuities are an insurance product, they offer a mechanism for insuring your future income. Other features (e.g., growth, tax-deferral, account access) should sound familiar when compared to other investment options you may have considered in your past.

Since you are likely accustomed to being able to withdraw money from your accounts (and perhaps were fearful that this would be impossible with an annuity), let's review what you can do with withdrawals first.

Withdrawals

"I have all the money I'll ever need, if I die by four o'clock." Henry Youngman

When considering withdrawals from an annuity, you will need to understand what is possible during the deferral years when you are accumulating value, versus what is possible in the payout years when you are taking money from your annuity.

The deferral or accumulation years are defined by the term of your contract. When you buy an annuity, you will select the term based on when you think you will need the income and/or when you will reach retirement age. Since annuities offer tax-deferred growth, the IRS has some influence over the timing. Like other retirement plans (e.g., IRAs, 401ks and SEPs), the primary purpose of annuities is to plan for income during retirement. Uncle Sam encourages us to put money away for retirement by offering tax incentives. On the flip side of that coin, there are disincentives (i.e., tax penalties and sometimes contractual penalties) for withdrawing money before age 59 ½ from any of these types of accounts – annuities included.

When you invest in an annuity, the underlying objective is to sock that money away for future use. However, unexpected needs can flare up, and it's good to know that you can access your money if you have to. So, here are the rules.

Liquidity During the Deferral Years

During the deferral years, most contracts allow withdrawals of **5-10% each year** without contractual penalty – which provides ample liquidity for most needs. Keep in mind, however, that you will still owe taxes on your tax-deferred gain, plus Uncle Sam will charge a penalty for withdrawing money before age 59 ½. Many annuities provide an option for cashing out completely. But, again cashing out before age 59 ½ leads to IRS penalties, plus there could be contractual penalties for cashing out before the end of your term. If you are acquainted with other tax-deferred vehicles like IRAs, 401ks, or SEPs, then the IRS penalties will sound familiar.

Unlimited Withdrawals

At the end of your contractual term, you may take as much out as you like, whenever you like. Let me say that again. **Withdraw as much as you like, whenever you like!** Your withdrawals may be random or systematic, and you may choose the amount and frequency *without* **initiating income guarantees.** What's left in your account will continue to grow as defined by your fixed, variable, or indexed contract. After the term is up, if you want to cash out completely, no problem (and no penalties). Annuities allow withdrawals, like any other account. Remember that taxes may apply.

Tax Treatment of Withdrawals

The tax treatment of your withdrawals will depend on the source of funds you used for your initial deposit. If you used "qualified" funds (e.g., IRA, SEP, 401k) to buy your annuity, then your withdrawals will be fully taxable. If you used "non-qualified" or post-tax funds, only the gains are taxable. In this case, the entire withdrawal will be taxable until the gains are expended. Uncle Sam will get his chunk of change first. (NOTE: The IRS allows you to spread the tax burden over the years when you *annuitize* — an option which will be discussed later).

How Long Will Your Money Last?

This book is about creating a forever paycheck for a worry-free retirement, so let's explore how the **withdrawal method** might play out when planning your future income. Imagine that your IRA 3% fixed annuity is worth $500,000 when you are ready to retire at 60 years old. Let's say you're disciplined, and want to produce something like a paycheck, so you plan **a systematic withdrawal** of $20,000 per year adjusted for 3% inflation annually with a 28% tax rate. What's left in the account after each withdrawal will continue to grow at the 3% fixed annuity rate. How long will your money last in this scenario? You can track the trajectory in Figure 4. The well will run dry in the 21st year, when you are 80 years old.

This won't be a problem *as long as* (a) you die at or before age 80 or (b) you have other funds to live on. Otherwise, this could be a risky income strategy. With the pure **withdrawal model**, like you may have in a market-related portfolio, you accept the full risk that you could outlive your money.

Figure 4

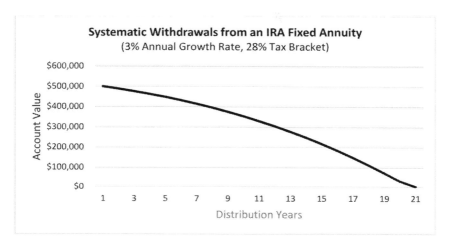

If you think that kind of exposure might make you worry about your future financial safety, then you will want to consider one of the paths annuities offer for guaranteed income. Income riders may be a good option in this case.

Income Riders

"In the business world, the rear view mirror is always clearer than the windshield." Warren Buffett

One of the most powerful tools you'll have at your disposal when developing your forever paycheck strategy is the income rider.

An **income rider is an optional perk** that can be attached to many annuities. It offers you a **guaranteed minimum income benefit** – while allowing you to **maintain access to your principal**. Income riders may provide a guaranteed growth rate, called a *roll-up rate*, which can be used for income, flexibility, and safety from a planning standpoint.

> **~ Lingo Alert ~**
> **Income Rider = Living Benefits = Guaranteed Minimum Income Benefit**
>
> When it comes to language, insurance companies can be their own worst enemy. Terms across firms are not necessarily standardized. So, you might hear different labels for the same thing. In the annuity world, income riders are sometimes called Living Benefits or Guaranteed Minimum Income Benefit (GMIB) riders. Same thing.

You choose to add an income rider when you initially purchase the annuity. You can't add it later, so remember your income objectives when you get started. Some annuities allow you to remove the rider later if you choose. Ask your financial advisor about the features associated with your contract and related costs.

It's Simply Insurance

When you get an income rider, you are buying income insurance. It's not that different from other forms of insurance you already have and understand. Look up the word "insurance" and you'll find definitions something like this: (1) an arrangement by which a company provides a guarantee of compensation for a specified loss, or (2) a thing providing protection against a possible eventuality. Insurance is the primary tool businesses and individuals use to reduce the financial impact of a risk occurring.

When you buy car insurance, for example, you are protecting yourself from the financial hardship that could occur after an accident or other vehicle-related incident. When you buy home insurance, you are protecting yourself from the financial hardship that could occur from a home-related incident. When you buy an income rider, you are protecting yourself from the financial hardship of an income-related "incident" – such as a poorly performing market or outliving your savings. In all three cases, you have a contract that defines how the insurance "pays out." You buy insurance *just in case* you need it.

Figure 5: Insurance

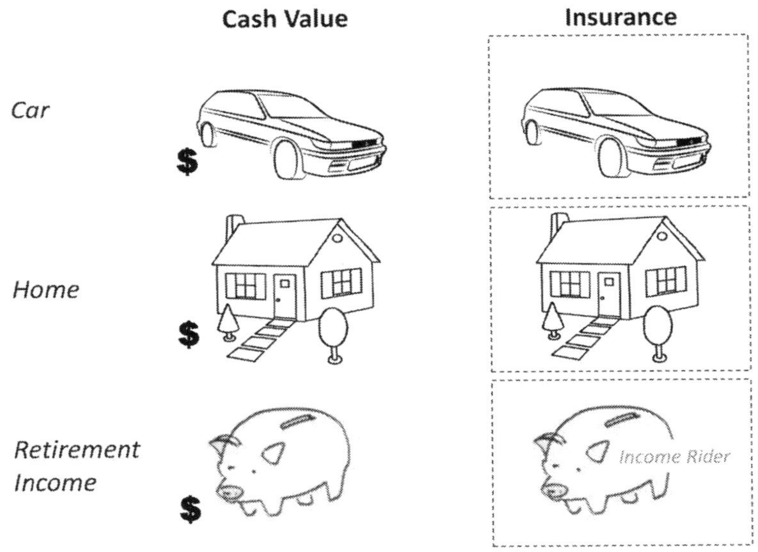

| Cash Value | Insurance |

Car

Home

Retirement Income

Income Rider

Guarantee on Top of a Guarantee

The best way to understand an income rider is to picture two buckets of value. The first bucket – we'll call it the **investment bucket** – contains the money you put into your deferred annuity. It grows at the rate defined in your fixed, variable, or indexed contract – whichever you selected when you purchased the annuity. This is your **cash accumulation account**.

Figure 6

Two Buckets of Value

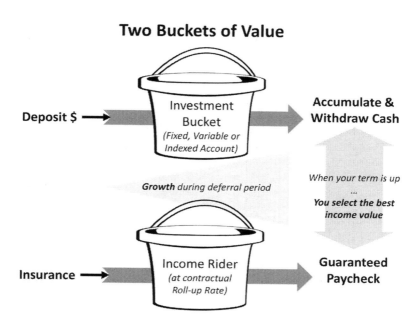

Now pause for a minute and consider this scenario. Let's say that, after reading the market tea leaves and considering your personal risk profile, you decide that a 10 year variable annuity is the one for you. You put $100,000 into this investment bucket and wait. Fast forward 10 years. The market was a weaker than expected over those 10 years, plus you decide to retire in the middle of a bear market. As it turns out, your variable account value has only grown 2.5%. In hind sight, it would have been better to get a 4% fixed annuity instead. In the standard investing world (e.g., if you had simply purchased a mutual fund), you would have to chalk that up to bad luck. But, *wouldn't it be great if* you could activate the super-secret back-up plan, pull out the trump card, hit the proverbial reset button, and choose the return that a 4% fixed annuity would have offered you instead?

Well, that's basically what an income rider does. The *income rider* is **your back-up bucket**. It provides a growth profile which is different from the one you selected in your investment bucket. At the end of your term, **you get to select the bucket with the highest value for income**.

It's like having sister accounts that grow side by side for a period of time defined by you. When that time is up, you get to have a beauty contest and pick a winner.

Slick, huh? What's the catch? The small catch is that the **income rider bucket can only be used for guaranteed income payments spread out over time**. You still own the investment bucket which contains your liquid funds, but you can't "cash out" the value in the income rider bucket like you can cash out of the investment bucket. When your term is up, and you are ready to create a forever paycheck, you will decide which bucket provides the more attractive income model.

An income rider allows you to transfer risk to the insurance company to pay you a forever paycheck starting at some point in the future. In exchange for taking this risk, the insurance company asks you to spread that money over time for future income versus withdrawing it all at once.

Before we get any more complex, look at the example in the diagram below. The left column shows stock market performance[20] between the years of 2000 and 2010. The middle column — your **investment bucket** — shows how an indexed annuity with a 5% cap and downside protection would have performed during this period. At the end of the term, you can take the money out of this investment bucket, pay taxes on the gain, and do something else with the balance.

Figure 7: Income Rider as a Back-Up Plan

	"Investment Bucket" (Accumulation Account)		"Back-up Bucket" (Income Rider)	
	A) Invested in the Market*		B) Indexed Annuity with downside protection with 5% growth cap		Income Rider at 4% guarantee	

Year	Stock Market Return	Account Value	Average Return	Account Value	Average Return	Account Value
Starting Point		$ 100,000.00		$ 100,000.00		$ 100,000.00
2000	-9.11%	$ 90,890.00	0.00%	$ 100,000.00	4.00%	$ 104,000.00
2001	-11.98%	$ 80,001.38	0.00%	$ 100,000.00	4.00%	$ 108,160.00
2002	-22.27%	$ 62,185.07	0.00%	$ 100,000.00	4.00%	$ 112,486.40
2003	28.72%	$ 80,044.62	5.00%	$ 105,000.00	4.00%	$ 116,985.86
2004	10.82%	$ 88,705.45	5.00%	$ 110,250.00	4.00%	$ 121,665.29
2005	4.79%	$ 92,954.44	4.79%	$ 115,530.98	4.00%	$ 126,531.90
2006	15.74%	$ 107,585.47	5.00%	$ 121,307.52	4.00%	$ 131,593.18
2007	5.46%	$ 113,459.64	5.00%	$ 127,372.90	4.00%	$ 136,856.91
2008	-37.22%	$ 71,229.96	0.00%	$ 127,372.90	4.00%	$ 142,331.18
2009	27.11%	$ 90,540.40	5.00%	$ 133,741.54	4.00%	$ 148,024.43
2010	14.87%	$ 104,003.76	5.00%	$ 140,428.62	4.00%	$ 153,945.41

Source of returns: MoneyChimp.com
Illustration does not include trading costs or fees.

On the far right, you see an **income rider** bucket with a 4% guarantee. **This is your "back-up" plan. It's** *insurance.* If the market is strong, the Indexed Annuity with a 5% cap will likely win the race. But, if the market performs like it did in this 10-year sampling, the income rider will prevail.

Look what happened in our example. The income rider applied a guaranteed 4% roll-up rate to the original $100,000. Over the years, the value of the back-up plan grew to $153,945.41 — almost 10% higher than the indexed annuity in your investment bucket.

At the end of your term, you get to choose. Which bucket seems more attractive for future income? Behind door number one: You can withdraw random amounts or a lump sum from your investment account worth $140,428.62, pay taxes on the gains, and move on. Behind door number two: You can initiate a guaranteed income stream from a base of $153,945.41. Granted, you can't walk away with that money in one lump sum, but you *can* start a forever paycheck which will be higher from this higher base than it would have been from your investment bucket. Super back-up plan!

There's actually a third option as well: You can use your investment account for a while, get a feel for your income requirements, and activate your income guarantee later. In this case, the value of your income rider bucket will be reduced by the same percentage that you reduce your investment bucket. So, if you withdraw 10% from your investment bucket, then the value of your income bucket will also go down 10%. Fair is fair.

Depending on your circumstances, any of these options could be attractive for different reasons. **The real value is having *a choice!***

I want to emphasize that last point before diving into more details of income riders. **Income riders are optional**. You *do not have to* attach an income rider to your annuity when you purchase it. Furthermore, if you *do* decide to attach an income rider, you *don't* have to turn it into a guaranteed income stream when your term is up. Even if you decide to activate the income rider and turn it into income, you *don't* have to "annuitize" it, so you will still have options. (NOTE: Annuitization is an optional, but irrevocable, process we will describe later). Therefore, an annuity with an income rider allows you to:

- Leave your money alone and let it grow inside of your investment account.
- Withdraw money in random amounts.
- Turn your paycheck on and off as you see fit.

So, again ... if you had any lingering concerns that you would somehow lose control of your money, an income rider can offer flexibility. For most contemporary annuities, an **income rider is an option** for guaranteeing you a **forever paycheck – without giving up principal access**. It offers a safety net by providing "sister accounts" which grow during the deferral years — the first one accumulating cash like a traditional investment, and the second one acting like an insurance plan accumulating value for future income. In this respect an **income rider offers you a second-chance potential for higher income**.

If and when you choose to activate the rider, you will receive regular payments at a payout rate guaranteed by the rider, based on your age when you activate. You can rely on these payments for the rest of your life (and spouse's life if you choose that option) — even if the market crashes or you live beyond the value in your account. The only thing that could reduce these payments would be your decision to withdraw money from your account value. In this case, your income rider account (and related paychecks) will be diminished by the same percentage. [NOTE: Some variable annuity contracts may limit access to the account value once you activate the income rider guarantees.]

An Example from Real Life

When Jim and Karen decided to retire, the market was in the midst of a full-blown decline. Ten years prior, they had put $375,000 into a variable annuity, selecting the funds that they thought would perform the best. Over the years, the account value had risen and fallen with the market. But, when they were ready to retire, the news wasn't favorable. Their account was only worth $350,000. Luckily, they had also purchased an income rider to insure their future income, and the value

---

of the income rider was $750,000. Had they invested in similar mutual funds without the security offered by insurance, Jim and Karen would have been forced to use the smaller $350,000 account value to fund their retirement. However, because the income rider guaranteed their future income, they were able to use the higher base of $750,000 to generate paychecks for life. In this case, an investment in insurance was well worth it.

Four Key Components

When considering an income rider you will want to understand four key components which together drive value.

- **Roll-up rate** — the name for income rider growth guarantees
- **Period** — the period of time for which the income rider is guaranteed
- **Payout percentage** — the factor the insurance company will use to determine the amount of your forever paycheck
- **Fees** (if any) associated with the income rider

As we walk through these value drivers, keep your eye on the ball. Remember, **maximizing your future income is your primary objective.** An income rider exists for one purpose – to supply future **lifetime income**, at a **guaranteed rate**, with more **flexibility** than traditional annuitization (discussed in the next chapter).

Roll-Up Rate

The growth rate on the income rider, called **the roll-up rate**, tells you how much your income rider bucket will grow each year during deferral. Products vary, so find out whether the roll-up rate offered will be compound or simple interest. Some annuities even sweeten the pot by offering upfront bonuses to enhance the starting value of the income rider bucket. For example, at the time of this writing, one annuity is offering a 4% bonus – so your income account would be credited with $4,000 for every $100,000 put into the annuity, giving you positive growth from day one.

It's important to understand the distinction between an income rider's guaranteed roll-up rate and the growth rate you receive in the investment bucket.

A common misunderstanding is to think of the income rider roll-up rate as a "yield", like you might receive in a bank account or CD. But the income rider isn't a bank account – it's insurance. If you have an income rider guaranteed to grow at 4% per year, it means that you will be able to use the gains for *future income*. It does not mean that you can walk away with this big lump sum in the future to go buy a Lamborghini. **The income rider dollar amount can only be used for income**. Meanwhile, your investment account — which you still own — is different. In this case, you *can* walk away with the money (although a Lamborghini might not be the best use). Naturally, if you walk away with your investment money, the value of your income rider account will fall to zero as well.

Period

The income rider roll-up rate will be guaranteed for a specific period of time during the deferral years.

Periods and nuances differ from product to product. To give you an idea of the range of possibilities, below are a few snapshots from annuities on the market today.

- **Guaranteed for the life of the contract or to a certain age**: For example, one product offers a 4% simple interest income rider that allows you to defer until you activate your income stream, or up to age 95.

- **Guaranteed for a specific period of time, then reset**: For example, an income rider could guarantee a 4% annual rate for the first nine deferral years, then renew at different rate at or above a particular floor like 3%.

- **Income riders with restrictions on when you can start your income stream**: For example, you might be required to defer for a set time frame before you are allowed to activate your income stream. There may even be limitations on which month of the year you can begin your forever paycheck. Some contracts require you to wait until the anniversary date, while others have no such constraints.

- **Income riders which increase the income value during the distribution stage to keep up with inflation.**

There are many possibilities across insurance carriers, so be sure to explore the period options and implications with your financial advisor.

The Payout (The Reason You're Reading this Book!)

Since your primary objective with an income rider is future income, pay keen attention to the payout structure (called "actuarial payout" in insurance terms). The payout is the **percentage the insurance company applies** to the income rider value to **determine the amount of your forever paycheck**. Let me say that more directly: **This rate tells you how big your check will be!**

The payout rate will depend on your age when you start your forever paycheck. As you might imagine, the younger you are when you start, the lower the payout (because the longer the insurance company will have to pay). The older you are, the higher the payout.

The table below offers *one example* of an actuarial payout for an annuity on the market today. Offerings vary, so talk to your financial advisor to evaluate payout rates for the products you are considering.

Figure 8: Sample Payout Structure

Attained Age at the Time of Election	Income Percentage	
	Single Annuitant	Joint Annuitants*
50-54	4.0%	3.5%
55-59	4.5%	4.0%
60-64	5.0%	4.5%
65-69	5.5%	5.0%
70-74	6.0%	5.5%
75-79	6.5%	6.0%
80-84	7.0%	6.5%
85-89	7.5%	7.0%
90+	8.0%	7.5%

*Based on the age of the younger annuitant. Joint Annuitants must be spouses.
Taxable amounts withdrawn prior to age 59 ½ may be subject to a 10% IRS penalty.

Payout Trumps Roll-Up Rate

Most of us are conditioned by the media to consider the percentage growth rate as the Holy Grail. However, in this case, income is your primary objective, so don't be too dazzled by the sizzle of a high rate. A larger income payout is what you want. And as counterintuitive as this may sound, a higher growth rate doesn't necessarily translate into a higher percentage income payout.

Remember, income riders are *insurance*. While a roll-up rate (i.e., growth rate) is an important consideration, it's not the end game – lifetime income is! For example, say you activate your forever paycheck from the 4% income rider bucket described in our earlier example (see Figure 7). At the end of the term this sample income account value was $153,945.41. If your payout percentage is 6%, then you will receive $9,236.72 per year for the rest of your life. But what if that same 4% income rider offered you a payout percentage of 5% at the same age? Your forever paycheck would only be $7,697.27 per year. Which annuity would you want? Even though the income rider in these two examples offered the same roll-up rate (i.e., 4%), the different actuarial payouts completely changed the end game for you. Since the whole purpose of the annuity is to offer you an income for the rest of your life, the actuarial payout rate is often more important than the growth rate in determining value.

Even within the same annuity, the payout structure should influence your decisions. For instance, take a look at the sample payout structure in Figure 8. If you are 64 1/2 years old when you start thinking about activating your forever paycheck, it would behoove you to wait another 6 months if possible — because doing so adds another 1/2 percentage point to the payout. Sticking with our example, waiting a few months would mean the difference between an annual forever paycheck of $7,697.27 starting at age 64 1/2 versus $8,465.00 at age 65.

Pay careful attention to your choices regarding single versus joint annuitant. On the surface, you may be tempted by the higher payout percentages shown for a single annuitant. However, you must realize that this choice will provide payments for your life alone. If you pass away before your spouse, your spouse could be left without sufficient income. A financial advisor can be helpful when it comes time to consider the options.

An Example from Real Life

Nancy (age 72) and Alan (age 78) were retired with $550,000 in total funds. Their mortgage was paid off and they were debt-free. In order to

---

cover their cost of living, they calculated that they would need $30,000 per year in lifetime income to combine with their social security income. Nancy and Alan asked me and another financial advisor to prepare quotes. We chose the same annuity with the highest payout in the early years.

The first advisor focused on Nancy and Alan's stated target without giving it a second thought. He proposed a $450,000 annuity for Alan (age 78) with a **SINGLE** life payout of $30,000, starting immediately. On the surface, this seemed like a perfect solution since it met Nancy and Alan's $30,000 income target exactly.

I suggested an alternative strategy which would provide financial security for both Alan and Nancy. I advised them to purchase $400,000 annuity, **deferring** income for 3 years, for a **JOINT** payout of $29,635 increasing to $30905 over the next 7 years. This option would **guarantee income for BOTH of their lifetimes**. To cover their needs during the 3 year deferral period, I suggested that they use $100,000 of their remaining nest egg to bridge the gap. This would leave them with approximately $50,000 in savings after the third year as a cushion for emergencies if needed.

If Alan and Nancy had chosen the first option with a SINGLE payout, Nancy's future security would have been left to chance. If Alan were to pass away in 5-6 years, Nancy would get a lump sum payment as the surviving spouse; however, the remaining account value would be approximately $300,000. Converting this remaining value into an income stream after Alan's death would only provide Nancy with $15,000-17,000 per year for the rest of her life. Alternatively, Nancy could decide to withdraw $30,000 annually from her remaining funds – but, in this case, Nancy's money would only last 5-7 more years.

The Joint payout was the safest way to ensure roughly $30,000 *payments per year spanning both of their lives. With this structure, any balance left in the account after both Nancy and Alan pass away would go to their heirs.*

Carefully designing a plan with your financial advisor can make all the difference.

Payout offerings vary. Some annuities encourage you to defer longer by providing better payout rates for longer terms. For example, one annuity on the market today increases the payout rate annually regardless of your growth rate. For example, $100,000 payout could be 4% if you hold the annuity for 3 years, but 8% if you hold it for 10 years — depending on your age. If you were planning your future income stream, an 8% payout potential would certainly grab your attention, because it produces a significantly larger forever paycheck. Other annuities offer an increasing income benefit, which allow you to withdraw increasing amounts from year to year.

The main point here is that the payout rate is actually more important than the roll-up rate when planning your forever paycheck, and it should be your number one driver when making an income rider decision. Talk to your financial advisor to determine what's most appropriate for your retirement needs.

Starting Your Forever Paycheck

When you decide to activate your income rider and begin your forever paychecks, the amounts will be deducted from your investment account's actual value. As long as you live, income payments will continue regardless of the underlying account value – even if it drops below your initial deposit plus gains. If there is a remaining balance in your accumulation value when you pass away, designated beneficiaries will receive it.

Using the same example, pretend you decide to convert your $153,945.41 income rider into forever paychecks when you're 60 at a 5% payout for a single annuitant ($7,697.27 per year). Figure 9 shows how this would work. The columns on the left show how your accumulation account value would change over time. For simplicity, I assumed that the market performance repeats the same historical pattern as our earlier example each decade. Your accumulation account will continue to grow per your contractual agreement (in this case, it's an indexed annuity with a 5% cap). Each year the amount of the forever paycheck will be subtracted from the value of this account until the account is depleted.

The accumulation account value is what your heirs would inherit if you pass away before the account is depleted at age 85. If you were to live to 93, you would continue to receive guaranteed payments – even though your investment account has been depleted – but, there would not be anything left in the investment account for your heirs to inherit after age 85. (Note: Example excludes tax impacts).

Regarding taxation, some annuities are **purchased with after-tax dollars**, so Uncle Sam already has his chunk of change from the **principal** — and you **won't be taxed again** on that portion of any withdrawal. The **gains will be taxed as ordinary income** (not capital gains). If you make random withdrawals from your account, your withdrawals will be fully taxable until the total amount of your investment gain has been withdrawn. If you decide to annuitize (discussed in the next chapter), then your principal and interest will be blended for lower taxation.

Figure 9: Accumulation Account Value with Forever Paycheck

	"Investment Bucket" (Accumulation Account)		Forever Paycheck	
	Indexed Annuity with downside protection with 5% growth cap		Income Rider - Converted into Lifetime Payments (5% payout)	
Age	Average Return	Account Value	Account Value	Paycheck
60		$ 140,428.62	$ 153,945.41	$ 7,697.27
61	0.00%	$ 132,731.35		$ 7,697.27
62	0.00%	$ 125,034.08		$ 7,697.27
63	0.00%	$ 117,336.81		$ 7,697.27
64	5.00%	$ 115,506.38		$ 7,697.27
65	5.00%	$ 113,584.43		$ 7,697.27
66	4.79%	$ 111,327.85		$ 7,697.27
67	5.00%	$ 109,196.97		$ 7,697.27
68	5.00%	$ 106,959.55		$ 7,697.27
69	0.00%	$ 99,262.28		$ 7,697.27
70	5.00%	$ 96,528.12		$ 7,697.27
71	5.00%	$ 93,657.26		$ 7,697.27
72	0.00%	$ 85,959.99		$ 7,697.27
73	0.00%	$ 78,262.72		$ 7,697.27
74	0.00%	$ 70,565.45		$ 7,697.27
75	5.00%	$ 66,396.45		$ 7,697.27
76	5.00%	$ 62,019.00		$ 7,697.27
77	4.79%	$ 57,292.44		$ 7,697.27
78	5.00%	$ 52,459.79		$ 7,697.27
79	5.00%	$ 47,385.51		$ 7,697.27
80	0.00%	$ 39,688.24		$ 7,697.27
81	5.00%	$ 33,975.38		$ 7,697.27
82	5.00%	$ 27,976.88		$ 7,697.27
83	0.00%	$ 20,279.61		$ 7,697.27
84	0.00%	$ 12,582.34		$ 7,697.27
85	0.00%	$ 4,885.07		$ 7,697.27
86				$ 7,697.27
87				$ 7,697.27
88				$ 7,697.27
89				$ 7,697.27
90				$ 7,697.27
91				$ 7,697.27
92				$ 7,697.27
93				$ 7,697.27

If you purchase your annuity with **pre-tax dollars** (as in an IRA, SEP or 401k), then your **entire withdrawal will be taxable**.

How Can They Do This?

At this point, you may be asking yourself, "How can an insurance company afford to offer this kind of guarantee with so many unknowns?" It boils down to statistics, probabilities, and math. Insurance companies know the odds and can spread their risks. Some people will live longer than average, others won't. The people who pass away early help pay for the people who live a long life.

An individual can't spread personal longevity risk. **Each of us has one roll of the dice, so it's prudent to make the most conservative bet and count on living a long time.**

Still, nothing is free. Insurance companies will cover their costs either by charging fees or offering returns slightly below what they believe they can earn on their own. They have time on their side. As long as you have money in your investment account, the insurance company has an opportunity to earn additional points on top of your investment.

Fees

Income Riders may or may not come with fees. For example, an income rider with a 6% growth rate guaranteed for 10 years of deferral might come at a fee of 0.95% per year. This rider fee is taken out of the investment bucket, not the income rider bucket, so it has an impact on accumulation value in your investment account without impacting the value of your income account. There are a few income riders that grow at a smaller rate, like 4.5%, during the deferrals years which do not charge fees. This is a long way of saying — do the math! Higher rates with fees could be better or worse than lower rates without fees.

Given that income riders may cost money, paying for one could make sense if your primary focus is on maximizing future income – because that's what an income rider insures. If you're sure that you'll want to cash out at the end of the term, then it might not make sense to "buy insurance" on your future income. For the purposes of this book, we're assuming that you're interested in creating income for a worry-free retirement, so the income rider is one viable option.

Here's one more note about fees. In the future, you may have a different idea than you have today about when you want to start your forever paycheck. Some riders allow you to renew or restart if you decide that you want to further delay your income stream. For example, imagine you have an income rider with a 6% annual rate, guaranteed for 10 years of deferral, at a 0.95% annual fee. When you purchased the annuity, perhaps you planned to retire at 60. But now you're 60, and you want to delay your income stream until you're 70. Your contract might provide an option for you to renew for another 10 years at that rate, while allowing the insurance company to charge a higher fee not to exceed a certain percentage, say 1.25%. It's important to be aware of these finer points, because a lot can happen in 10 years. Your current advisor may or may not be in the picture in 10 years, and the annuity company may or may not have a great process for reminding you. The income rider won't automatically renew simply because you decide to wait for a while. You have to tell the provider that's what you want to do.

Take Your Time to Consider the Benefits

There are many income rider choices out there. All have different rules, guarantees, and functions. Take your time, collect the facts, and discuss the options with your financial advisor to pick an option that's right for you.

Incomer riders are designed to ensure that you will have a reliable income for life. This is their unique function. With most other retirement plans, you can outlive your income. Many other investments leave you exposed to market volatility where your savings can go down the tubes when the market tanks, upping the risk that your income will run dry. In contrast, an annuity with an income rider can offer:

- **Investment flexibility**: You can choose the growth profile, risk tolerance and time horizon that suits you best.
- **Back-up plan:** An income rider provides a second set of values to be used for future income which could outshine the performance of your traditional investment account. You get to choose the best option for your income.
- **Income flexibility**: You can choose if, when, and how to create your future income streams — ranging from random withdrawals from your investment account to systematic paychecks from your income account, or some combination of the two.
- **Access:** During the deferral years you typically may withdraw 5-10% without contractual penalties. (Remember IRS penalties will apply if you are under 59 ½). After the contractual term, called the surrender period, you may withdraw as much as you want without contractual penalty. Income tax may apply.
- **Control:** It's your annuity. You control the investment. You select the options. You control how and when to use your money.

If income riders aren't your thing, there is one more way to produce a forever paycheck — annuitization.

Annuitization

"There's no reason to be the richest man in the cemetery. You can't do any business from there." Colonel Harlan Sanders

Like everything else, **annuitization is a choice** — in some ways, an old fashioned choice. Decades ago when insurance carriers began to offer pension annuities, annuitization was your only choice. Today, annuities offer many more options, and annuitization is *one way* to create your forever paycheck. Before you choose this option, be sure you understand how the process works, as well as its long-term consequences.

How Does Annuitization Work?

When you decide to annuitize, you are telling the insurance company that you would like to **convert your deferred annuity into a guaranteed income stream.** Like an income rider, annuitization allows you to receive a specified income for life (or other predetermined period of time), however, the key difference is that annuitization is **an *irrevocable* decision.** Once you annuitize, the insurance company takes steps to guarantee your payments, and **you can't go back to change your income payout.**

Annuitization is a one-time event that occurs between the accumulation and payout stages. At this point, the insurance carrier uses a mathematical formula to convert your account's accumulation value into a monthly payout. The size of your forever paycheck will depend on:

- Your account value
- Current interest rates

- Your life expectancy and that of your beneficiaries (if any)
- The choices you make regarding how the annuity will be paid out (e.g., frequency, duration, additional benefits for spouses or heirs, etc.).

When you annuitize, you **give up access** to your account value in exchange for **guaranteed future income payments**. Depending on the payout options you select, residual account value could be forfeited to the insurance company upon your death. You can add more coverage (e.g., a second person, a specific time frame, benefits for your heirs, etc.), when you contract with the insurance company. As you might expect, more bells and whistles cost money – either in the form of fees or reduced future income streams. This is the insurance company's way of compensating for any additional risks it may assume.

The **payout** associated with annuitized contracts *can be* **higher** than other options — especially if you are planning income for your life only. So, by giving up something (i.e., access), you could gain something (i.e., more income). It's important to work with a financial professional, consider your personal circumstances, and **do the math** to compare annuitization to other options available to you.

Structuring Your Payments

When you annuitize, you will have to decide how to structure the payments. Your optimum payment structure will depend on whether you have other sources of income, other people counting on the income, or other personal circumstances.

There are a variety of options, including:

- Lifetime payments

- Life with Period Certain
- Joint and Last Survivor
- Joint and Last Survivor with Period Certain
- Period Certain

These options probably sound like insurance gobbledygook, so let's break them down.

The **Lifetime Payments** option allows you to receive income payments for the rest of *your* life, regardless of how long (or short) that may be. This is the most straight-forward arrangement, providing income **for your life only**. If you die early, the insurance company will get to keep your money. If you live a long life and exhaust the value in your original account, the insurance company has to keep paying you until your death. The lifetime payment option might be a good choice if you're only taking care of yourself. If there are other people counting on the income or you want to leave an inheritance, you will want to look into the other options.

The **Life with Period Certain** option **pays you for life, plus provides a benefit to your heirs should you die early**. In other words, you sign up for a "certain" period, perhaps ten or twenty years. If you die within that time frame, your beneficiary will get the balance of your income payments for the period certain. If you live longer than that, no worries. *Your* payments will continue for life, no matter how long that may be — but your heirs opportunity will expire at the end of the period certain. For example, imagine that you have a $100,000 annuity and choose Life with a twenty-year Period Certain. The contract will be annuitized, paying you monthly. If you die in the fourth year, your beneficiaries will get whatever remains in your 20-year payout, paid out with the same payments you were getting, for another sixteen-years. If you live beyond the twenty-years, you continue to get the same payout until death, even if it exceeds your initial investment values. The *period certain* pertains to your beneficiaries – simply defining a *certain period of time* in which they may receive income benefits from your account if you die during that time frame.

The **Joint and Last Survivor** is designed to **ensure that both you and your spouse or other significant person will be covered for life.** This option makes payments to you and your spouse or to you and another designated party until you both have passed away. In other words, Joint and Last Survivor provides income spanning two lives, not one. This joint payout is often higher than other joint income options, however, it comes with a cost – if you both die early, the insurance company will get to keep your money.

Like Life with Period Certain, **Joint and Last Survivor with Period Certain** provides a benefit to your heirs if you and your spouse die before the "certain period." If you and/or your spouse live beyond the period certain, you continue to get the same payout until death, even if it exceeds your initial investment values. The "period certain" simply defines a span of time in which your beneficiaries may receive remaining income payments from your account if neither you nor your spouse remain here on earth.

The **Period Certain** option allows you to select a specific (i.e., "certain") period of time for which *your* income payments will last. This option usually provides a higher monthly payment than the life option, since it also offers more certainty to the insurance company. Of course, this small boost in income means that *you* are accepting the risk that your annuity payments will run out before your death. For example, say you decide to start your income stream when you're 65 years old, and choose a 15-year period-certain payout option. This will provide you with a retirement income until you're 80. Should you die at or before age 80, this option would not present a problem. But if you live longer than 80 years and do not have another source of retirement income, this option would be dicey.

The Most Common Misconception

The kinds of restrictions associated with annuitization often falsely scare investors away from annuities. **Thinking that annuitization is a *default* requirement is a common <u>misconception</u>**. In fact, many annuity holders never annuitize, opting instead to use the annuity to create a forever paycheck. A 2005 Gallup survey of non-qualified annuity owners revealed that only 17% had opted to annuitize their contracts[21]. And that percentage may be even lower today. Recent sources estimate that less than 10% of all annuities are actually annuitized[22].

Is Annuitization A Good Strategy?

The main reason to annuitize is because you want the guaranteed payments, and you find that it offers a higher income payout for your situation. If you are not worried about relinquishing control of the account and want to maximize your forever paycheck, then annuitization might make sense for you. One factor to consider when evaluating your options is how much money you have saved in other assets (i.e., outside the annuity contract). If you have other significant sources of liquid savings, then annuitization may be a suitable choice because you can draw on other assets in the event of an emergency. Clearly, it would not be wise to tie all of your savings up in an irrevocable cash flow, even if it would maximize return on investment.

Financial advisors can help you explore hybrid strategies as well.

For example, a married couple might be able to optimize payout and forfeiture risk by supplementing a straight joint-life payout with a term insurance policy that will pay out a tax-free death benefit to the survivor. If you no longer need a life insurance policy with cash value, you might consider transferring your full basis, including premiums and cash value, to an annuity. This allows you to maintain tax deferral benefits on interest earned. Work with a professional to examine the cost-benefit impact of your options before making a final decision.

If you choose *not* to annuitize your contract, you have several other options.

- You can liquidate your contract at no cost (other than taxes) at age 59 ½ or older, provided that the surrender charge schedule on your contract has expired.
- You can keep the account and pass the account balance to your beneficiaries as a death benefit (taxes may apply).
- Or you can roll your contract into another annuity and continue to grow your funds tax deferred.

If you want access to your principal in addition to receiving lifetime income, you will probably find an income rider to be more appealing. **Income riders are a popular alternative to annuitization** because they provide an income guarantee that often exceeds the contract's accumulation value without locking you into an irrevocable payout schedule. One great thing about an income rider is that you can plan ahead for a future income stream and still decide to annuitize later if your objectives, circumstances and math point in that direction. An income rider gives you this flexibility.

~ Lingo Alert ~
Annuity does not equal Annuitized

I'm convinced that most of the confusion about annuities stems from language. I'm no linguist, but through the years I have come to believe that verbs and nouns with the same stem go together. For example, an "investment" (noun) is "invested" (verb) — Right? Off the top of my head, I can't think of a situation where I would argue that an investment isn't invested. So, wouldn't that mean that "annuities" are "annuitized?"

No. An annuity is not necessarily annuitized. It's simply one of the two options for converting your annuity into guaranteed lifetime income. The other option is an income rider. I'll have to consult with a linguist on this, but perhaps we need a verb like "income-ridered." If you want income guarantees, your annuity will need to be annuitized or income-ridered. You get to choose. Don't let Webster get in the way.

Immediate Income

"Your big opportunity might be right where you are now." Napoleon Hill

Typically, annuities are used for "deferred" income – meaning that you invest today in order to create income for retirement several years into the future. What if you are already retired or moments from it, you don't own an annuity yet, but you need a forever paycheck to mitigate the risk of outlasting your money? It's not too late.

You can purchase an annuity designed to provide immediate income with the same features we have discussed so far — including the option to select an income rider which allows you to maintain access to your principal.

While many options are possible, industry experts generally use the term "Immediate Annuity" to refer to a Single Premium Immediate Annuity (or "SPIA", pronounced spee-uh) — so named because it is purchased with a single, lump sum called a premium. **Payments start right away and continue for the rest of your life** or other specified period of time. SPIAs are annuitized products.

In return for your lump sum, the insurance company agrees to make regular payments to you (or to a payee you specify) for the time frame you selected– usually for life, however long that may be. The frequency of your payments are up to you. Most people choose to receive monthly payments, but you could choose quarterly or even yearly if that suits you better. It's your choice.

When it comes to guaranteeing income for life, **immediate annuities often beat other options.** Remember — an SPIA is an annuitized product. In exchange for a payment guarantee, you relinquish access to your original premium. You are generally *unable* to revise or cash in an immediate annuity.

Perhaps this sounds morbid, but here's how it works. You are betting that you will have a long life span. The insurance company is betting that you will have an average life span. The insurance company is able to provide this guarantee – no matter how long you live – because they can spread their risk across many lives basing their assumptions on statistics. Some people will live longer than average, and the insurance company will have to pony up more than the original premium plus growth. Other people will depart this life sooner than expected and leave some money on the table. If you are the immediate annuity owner, you're betting that you will beat the odds and be the one to enjoy a long life. Plus, you are mitigating the risk that you could otherwise outlive your income.

Before you reject the idea of potentially leaving some money on the table when you meet your maker, consider the benefits. An immediate annuity comes with many important advantages. Here are a few:

- **Peace of Mind**. The annuity provides stable income for life. You will never fear outliving your savings.
- **Freedom**. Once it's set, all you have to do is collect your forever paycheck. You won't need to watch markets or track interest rates and dividends.
- **Higher Returns**. The interest rates used by insurance companies to calculate income from an immediate annuity are generally higher than CD or Treasury rates.
- **Safety.** Funds in your immediate annuity are guaranteed by insurer assets, in a highly regulated industry, and are not subject to financial markets fluctuations.
- **No sales or administrative charges**. There are no annual account management or maintenance charges associated with an immediate annuity. A full 100% of your premium goes towards your monthly income.
- **Potential for more income.**

Consider this example. Say Joe Investor is 60 and ready to retire. He has a $500,000 nest egg and needs income right away. What are his safest options? You can track the options in the Figure 10.

Certificate of Deposit: He could invest in the example CD offering a return of 2.25% per year. Since he needs immediate income, he might decide to start with a 4% or $20,000 distribution during the first year (we'll share more on the 4% rule in a later chapter) adjusted by 3% each year for inflation. As you can see in the following table, the CD scenario shows he would run out of money at age 84.

Figure 10: Safe Money Options

Age	2.25% CD		3% Bonds		Immediate Annuity
	Withdrawal at Start of Year	Nest Egg at Start of Year	Withdrawal at Start of Year	Nest Egg at Start of Year	Withdrawal at Start of Year
60	$20,000	$500,000	$20,000	$500,000	$29,984
61	$20,600	$490,800	$20,600	$494,400	$29,984
62	$21,218	$480,780	$21,218	$488,014	$29,984
63	$21,855	$469,902	$21,855	$480,800	$29,984
64	$22,510	$458,128	$22,510	$472,714	$29,984
65	$23,185	$445,419	$23,185	$463,710	$29,984
66	$23,881	$431,734	$23,881	$453,740	$29,984
67	$24,597	$417,030	$24,597	$442,755	$29,984
68	$25,335	$401,262	$25,335	$430,702	$29,984
69	$26,095	$384,385	$26,095	$417,527	$29,984
70	$26,878	$366,351	$26,878	$403,175	$29,984
71	$27,685	$347,111	$27,685	$387,585	$29,984
72	$28,515	$326,613	$28,515	$370,698	$29,984
73	$29,371	$304,805	$29,371	$352,448	$29,984
74	$30,252	$281,632	$30,252	$332,770	$29,984
75	$31,159	$257,036	$31,159	$311,593	$29,984
76	$32,094	$230,959	$32,094	$288,847	$29,984
77	$33,057	$203,339	$33,057	$264,456	$29,984
78	$34,049	$174,114	$34,049	$238,341	$29,984
79	$35,070	$143,217	$35,070	$210,421	$29,984
80	$36,122	$110,580	$36,122	$180,611	$29,984
81	$37,206	$76,133	$37,206	$148,824	$29,984
82	$38,322	$39,803	$38,322	$114,966	$29,984
83	$39,472	$1,514	$39,472	$78,943	$29,984
84	$1,514	$0	$40,656	$40,656	$29,984
85	$0	$0	$0	$0	$29,984
Total Withdrawals:	$690,043		$729,185		$779,584
Earnings Above Principal:	$190,043		$229,185		$279,584

NOTE: Taxes not considered in the equations above.

Bonds: He could invest in bonds, which the example above assumes would pay him 3% per year. Following the same logic, pretend he starts with a 4% or $20,000 distribution, adjusted by 3% each year for inflation. In this case, his money would run dry at age 85.

Immediate Annuity: He could deposit his $500,000 into an immediate annuity and begin receiving **lifetime** payments of $29,984 per year. Since the annuity is guaranteed to continue no matter how long he lives, Joe can live to 100 or beyond and the payments will continue long after the initial deposit is expended. Had he withdrawn this amount of income from any other account, without the income insurance provided by the Immediate Annuity, his $500,000 would have lasted about 17 years.

Notice the total withdrawals in our three examples (Figure 10). Over the course of 25 years, the CD would have paid Joe $690,043 ($190,043 above his original nest egg). Bonds would have paid $729,185 ($229,185 above his original nest egg). The Immediate Annuity would have paid Joe $779,584 in this time frame – already $279,584 above his original nest egg – and it's still going. As long as Joe is alive, this cumulative amount will continue to build.

While in the first two cases Joe would maintain complete control and access to his principal, he would potentially run out of money before he runs out of life. In the third case, the insurance company will pay him *more* for *longer* in exchange for rights to his initial deposit. Yes, if he dies early, the insurance company keeps the change. Joe will have to decide how much that matters to him. He can't take it with him anyway.

When faced with the quandary of how to insure your income stream in your later years, you will have to decide. Which is the better "return?"

Customizing an Immediate Annuity

When you shop for an immediate annuity, the price will be driven by your age, life expectancy and any extra benefits you decide to add to your contract. You can add some perks to your immediate annuity coverage by:

- Including a second person ("Joint and Survivor" annuity)
- Adding a guaranteed period of time ("Period Certain" annuity)

- Guaranteeing that payments will continue at least until the original purchase amount has been paid out so that your beneficiaries can receive any remaining balance if you die early.

However, because these extra benefits add risk for the insurer, there will be a cost. Monthly payments will likely be reduced by some amount, perhaps 5% to 15%, depending on the age (or ages) of the annuitant(s) and the duration of the guarantee period.

Which option is best?

"The choices we make are ultimately our own responsibility." Eleanor Roosevelt

The path you select for generating your forever paycheck will depend on several personal factors including health, projected longevity, financial circumstances, risk tolerance, investment objectives, liquidity needs, etc. Consider this example: Imagine Joe and Sally are married and about to retire at 65 and 62 years old. They decide to purchase a $100,000 indexed annuity designed to pay them immediate income and consider two choices for creating an income stream:

- **Option 1: An Income Rider** will guarantee a minimum of $5,000 per year until both of them have passed away – even after the accumulation value in the contract has been exhausted. Joe and Sally's heirs will receive what's left in their account as long as there is a balance. Plus, if the markets perform well, their payout could be slightly higher.
- **Option 2: Annuitization with a joint-life payout and 20-year period certain** will provide $5,297 per year until both Sally and Joe have passed away, and it allows their beneficiaries to receive their remaining payments if they both die within 20 years.

Which option is right? *It depends.* While the annuitized option will pay a higher monthly payment, Joe and Sally will relinquish control of their account, and the payout will be an irrevocable decision. If they have other liquid funds to cover surprise expenses in the future, this might be a perfectly acceptable trade-off to them.

The income rider, on the other hand, has a lower monthly payment but will allow Joe and Sally to maintain access to their accumulation value. If they need the money in the future for some reason — to pay medical expenses, purchase a car, help a family member, improve a home, or whatever — they can have it. If this is their primary source of income, the extra liquidity can make a big difference.

The right choice for the Joe and Sally will depend on their personal objectives and situation. The same will be true for you. Consider your options carefully and discuss the trade-offs with your financial advisor when making decisions about your forever paycheck.

6

Are Annuity Companies Safe?

"Trust, but verify." Ronald Reagan

Most investors in their prime earning years can recall a few financial institution melt-downs. You might remember the Savings and Loan (S&L) bailout of 1989. About half of America's S&Ls – more than 1,600 – failed between 1986 and 1995. Billions in federally-insured deposits had to be covered by the government.

Also fresh in our minds is the sub-prime mortgage disaster of 2007-2008, which brought giants like Bear Sterns, Fannie Mae, and Freddie Mac to their knees. In mid-September 2008, the U.S. government took control of American International Group (AIG), one of the world's largest insurance companies. The federal government guaranteed to loan AIG up to $85 billion, and in return took a 79.9% equity position in AIG. It's important to note that AIG's troubles had nothing to do with its insurance division, but rather stemmed from losses on bad derivative bets. In fact, AIG's hefty insurance revenues[23] made the company a safe bet for the U.S. government.

Considering these visible industry examples, it's not surprising that most of us are concerned about the safety and strength of the financial institutions we engage. Annuity guarantees – including income riders – are only as good as the company backing them. So, it's wise to look under the covers before handing your hard earned money to any financial institution.

Historically, annuities have proven to be one of the safest strategies for your money. Remember Babe Ruth, who enjoyed a worry free retirement *even in the dark of the Great Depression* because of annuities! Nevertheless, wanting to know more about the strength of your annuity provider is a healthy question, so let's dig in.

Highly Regulated Industry

The first thing you will want to know is that the insurance industry is **highly regulated to protect policyholders**. Insurance companies must be licensed in each state in which they operate and be members of the state's guaranty association. This provides a mechanism backing each other up in the event of failure. In addition, they are required to maintain sufficient reserves to meet the majority of their obligations to policyholders. State insurance departments continually monitor members' financial stability. According to the National Organization of Life & Health Insurance Guaranty Associations[24] (NOLHGA) since 1983, state guaranty associations have:

- Provided protection to more than 2.5 million policyholders
- Guaranteed more than $22 billion in coverage benefits

- Contributed approximately $6.2 billion toward the fulfillment of insurer promises

The U.S. has a strict state regulation system to ensure that life insurance companies are adequately capitalized. That has kept the number of insolvencies to a minimal level

Industry Track Record

To give you some peace of mind, consider this. History has shown that insurance companies under financial duress are generally snapped up by competitors with policies and annuities transferring seamlessly — terms and guarantees intact. The insurance industry has a better track record than most industries when it comes to successful rehabilitations and liquidations. Over the past 30 years, the assets of at least 70 financially stressed life insurance companies taken over by state insurance departments were successfully redistributed[25]. Compare this to the number of Savings and Loans that failed in one decade, and it doesn't sound so scary.

Doing Your Homework

Following are a few resources you can use to evaluate the safety of the annuity industry and to assess the strength of your carrier. Experienced financial advisors will recognize these tools and be able to help you get answers.

State Guarantee Fund: State guaranty associations play a vital role in overseeing the insurance industry and protecting policyholders from insolvencies. Annuities are regulated and backed at the state level, and each state guarantees a specific dollar amount.

You can go to www.nolhga.com to find out what your state guarantees. All state guaranty associations provide a minimum of

$100,000 in benefit protection for annuities – regardless of the annuity's deferred or payout status at the time of insolvency. And most states (94%) provide at least $250,000 in protection. Furthermore, policy amounts above these protection levels are backed by the remaining assets in the insolvent company, which can be quite substantial.[26]

NOTE: You should know that state guarantees cover the accumulation value in your investment bucket only. They don't cover income rider valuations. This should not be an issue since your cash value is attached to your accumulation account anyway.

Ratings Services: Rating agencies for insurance carriers include Standard & Poors, Moody's, Fitch, A.M. Best, and Weiss. All are great resources when you are ready to research the strength of various carriers.

Carrier Balance Sheet: Take a look at the insurance carrier's balance sheet and fixed-income holdings. From an internal perspective, this gives you a picture of the assets which support the annuity policies.

Safety Strategies

In short, here are four actions you can take to put your mind at ease regarding safety:

1. Review multiple options with your financial advisor. Compare several products and carriers to find the one that suits your needs best.
2. Look at ratings from multiple rating agencies and review the carrier's balance sheet. Use these two indicators to select a strong carrier.

3. Check out guarantees offered at the state level and by the annuity provider, and buy within that range.

4. Diversify. Don't put *all* of your money into an annuity. Figure out which proportion of your money you want to reserve for safe future income and start there. Depending on your holdings and objectives, you might also want to consider diversifying your annuity portfolio across multiple carriers.

This advice is not unique to annuities. You would follow the same advice to assess the safety of other investment options too. For example, bonds are rated for safety as well. An investment grade bond beats a junk bond when it comes to safety. The headline for all investments — including annuities — is to do your homework before you plunk down your hard-earned cash.

If you let history be your guide and prudence be your partner, you'll find annuities to be a safe place to put your money and insurance companies to be worthy guardians.

7

Kiss the Dragons

"You can't take care of a threat that you are afraid to face. You have to kiss the dragon." Stan Aldrich, Friend and Mentor

Early in my career, I had a wonderful friend who had a favorite piece of advice. If he caught me avoiding a potentially threatening situation, he would say "You can't take care of a threat that you are afraid to face. You have to kiss the dragon." This was his way of encouraging me to fully investigate and understand any possible risk, so that I could develop an appropriate strategy for dealing with it. To this day, a quarter of a century later, I still think of his sage advice when faced with an unpleasant topic.

So, this chapter is about the "dragons" that can threaten your future income streams. I don't mean to be fear-mongering, but rather want to put the facts on the table as directly as I can so that we can openly consider strategies for mitigating the risks of being burned later on.

Income dragons for the retirement planner include:

- Hype around market indexes
- The myth of average returns
- Buy and hold impacts in retirement
- Income-eating inflation
- Risks of cognitive decline
- Misconceptions about annuities

You Can't Beat an Index

"I never attempt to make money on the stock market. I buy on the assumption that they could close the market the next day and not reopen it for ten years." Warren Buffett

Expecting to beat a market benchmark like an index is possibly the single biggest mistake that investors make. This is understandable considering that Wall Street has enticed us with unrealistic targets for years. We are conditioned by Wall Street and the media to believe that the best way to maximize returns is to put our money in the market. Headlines scream "The Dow Jones Industrial Average Soars!" or "The S&P 500 Hits Record Highs." We run to our account statements hoping to see that our balances have soared by the same impressive percentages, usually to be disappointed by an entirely less enthralling result.

Dalbar, the nation's leading financial services market research firm, consistently demonstrates that the average investor's twenty-year annualized return is shockingly low next to what the market tells us to expect. Here is a sound bite from their 2012 study, *Quantitative Analysis Of Investor Behavior:* Over the twenty year period ending Dec. 31, 2011, **the average investor earned 2.1%.** [27]

The Gulf Between Expectations and Reality

Over the same time frame, stock brokers and mutual fund providers would have undoubtedly pointed to the performance of the S&P 500 (which returned 7.8%) and the Barclays Capital U.S. Aggregate Bond Index (which returned 6.5%) as indicators of what could be expected from our investments. Theoretically, an investor with a perfectly balanced portfolio of these two asset classes would have earned 7.2%. Compare *that* to the 2.1% reality, and the gap is flabbergasting! In reality, the news is worse than that. After inflation, the average investor's return during that time frame was actually negative. The consumer price index (CPI) grew at an annualized rate of 2.5% during the same period. So the average investors' net real return was -0.4%.

Before we go much further, it's important to recognize that it's technically impossible for an investor to consistently *beat* an index.[28] Taxes, trading costs, and fees take a bite out of a normal investor's portfolio over time. In addition, there are subtleties in the calculation of the market capitalization weighted index that simply don't translate to an individual's dollar invested portfolio. If you are interested in learning more about the index, Lance Roberts explains these dynamics in his 2013 *StreetTalk* article, "Why You Can't Beat the Index."[28]

Even if we allow for taxes, trading costs, fees, and index calculation vagaries, experts say that these factors alone can't explain the typical investor's chronic under-performance over time. In 2014, Dalbar showed that the **average investor's earnings missed the market by 60-80%**:

- Average equity mutual fund investors **lagged the S&P 500 by 8.19 percentage points**. The S&P 500 earned 13.7%, while equity fund investors earned an average of 5.5%.
- Average fixed income mutual investors **missed the Barclays Aggregate Bond Index by 4.81 percentage points**. The broader bond market pulled in nearly 5.97%, while the average investor earned only 1.16%.

Suffice it to say that the odds of beating a market index are low. Why? Dalbar boils it down to two primary issues: psychology and capital. While costs (e.g., trading costs, fees, taxes) are important when comparing specific investment options; the emotional mistakes investors make over time are much more significant.

"What lies behind you and what lies in front of you, pales in comparison to what lies inside of you." Ralph Waldo Emerson

False expectations lead investors to jump from one investment strategy to another and one advisor to the next. Since moving money produces fees and commissions, these choices are great news for Wall Street, but bad news for you. Market returns are like the carrot dangled in front of the horse — constantly out of reach. If achieving index-level returns was your hope, then check your expectations. Beating, or even matching, an index is statistically unlikely and technically infeasible.

One thing you can control, however, is your own psychology. Most costly mistakes are made on the winds of emotion. Since you are the captain of your own ship, it's up to you to chart a practical course for the future and to manage your emotions along the way. Dalbar points to several irrational investment behaviors that can prevent you from meeting your goals:

- **Unrealistic Optimism:** Making overly optimistic assumptions, which lead investors to retreat when met with reality.
- **Herding:** Following the masses, which leads people to buy high and sell low.
- **Media Mania:** Buying into what the media is selling or sensationalizing.
- **Loss Aversion / Panic Selling:** Succumbing to fear of loss and withdrawing capital at the worst possible time.
- **Lack of Diversification** – Believing a portfolio is diversified when, in fact, it is a highly correlated pool of assets.
- **Regret Paralysis** – Not taking a necessary action because of regret from a previous failure.

Focus on Income

Dalbar's studies force us to think deeply about our expectations, habits, and commitments. No matter what your goals are, having the foresight to develop a plan and the tenacity to stick with it is job one. The clearer you are about your objectives, the better positioned you will be to make good decisions.

If you decide that lifetime income is important to you, then you are likely to bump into annuities on the menu of choices. Annuities are simply the **most certain path for ensuring future income.** They provide a mechanism for mitigating the risk that market performance gets in the way of your financial security. Yet, annuities are frequently the topic of impassioned debates about rates of return – usually starting with the assumption that the competitive option (i.e., the market) will deliver what the index implies.

It's difficult to compare investments with no guarantee (e.g., stocks, bonds, mutual funds, etc.) to an investment *with* a guarantee (e.g., annuities). It's not an apples to apples comparison. Nevertheless, value is important – so let's give it a try. The best way to understand the value delivered by an annuity versus non-guaranteed options is to break the exploration into two phases – **accumulation and distribution** – observing how money flows in and out over this entire two-stage lifecycle.

Accumulation

To examine an accumulation stage, let's reconstruct what would have happened to Joe Investor's $100,000 investment in a market mimicking the period between 1992 and 2011 (the two decades studied by Dalbar). Figure 11 shows you how the S&P 500 would have shaped investor expectations during this time versus the results the average investor *actually* realized.

Figure 11: Expectations Versus Reality

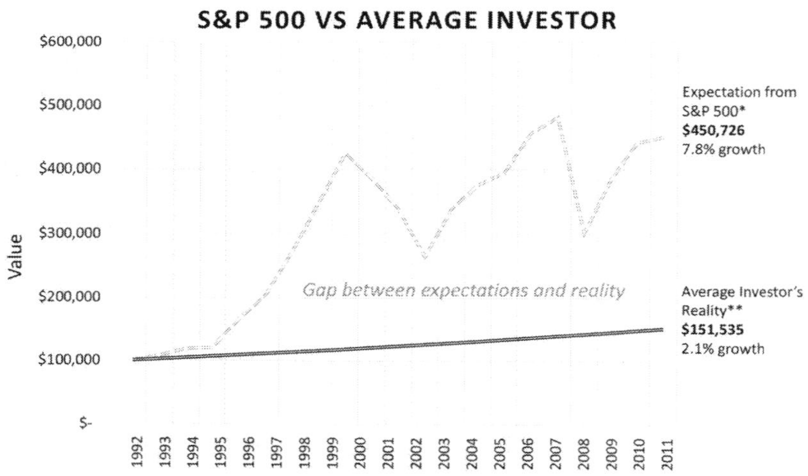

S&P 500 VS AVERAGE INVESTOR

Gap between expectations and reality

Expectation from S&P 500*
$450,726
7.8% growth

Average Investor's Reality**
$151,535
2.1% growth

* Annualized growth rate of the S&P 500 from moneychimp.com
** Average investor returns 1992-2011, Dalbar study
Excludes trading costs, fees and taxes.

The S&P 500 would have rambled along, with ups and downs as shown. After a few decades, the media and Wall Street would ring the bell and celebrate a 7.8% annualized growth rate. If Joe bought the hype, he probably would have expected his initial $100,000 investment to be worth $450,726.

In reality, Joe would have experienced a completely different result. Like other average investors, he would have had a smaller portfolio (versus all 500 companies in the S&P index) that wouldn't have tracked exactly to the index. He might have fallen victim to an occasional emotional demon and changed investment strategies. He would have sacrificed a chunk of change to trading costs, fees and taxes. At the end of the same twenty years, Joe would be licking his wounds with a 2.1% return and a portfolio value of $151,535 — wondering why his portfolio's performance was so far from Wall Street's mark. Granted, some of the poor result could have stemmed from his own decisions (psychology). But, some of the gap was merely fiction created by the hype around a market index.

Now, let's look at what would have happened if Joe had invested his $100,000 in an indexed annuity with a 5% cap.

Figure 12 shows the difference in account values during accumulation if Joe had invested his money in the indexed annuity versus achieving the average investor's results in the market.

The annuity path would have provided twice the average investor's profit with an ending value of $204,087— at a mild, but respectable, 3.6% return. His returns wouldn't have made the news like the S&P, but he would have benefited from market up-cycles without losing sleep or money during down cycles. Plus, he would have had a nest egg to turn into guaranteed income in the distribution stage – which is where an annuity can truly produce value.

Figure 12: Accumulation Stage

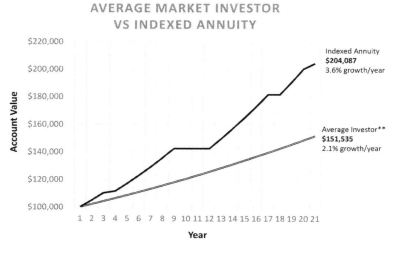

AVERAGE MARKET INVESTOR
VS INDEXED ANNUITY

Indexed Annuity
$204,087
3.6% growth/year

Average Investor**
$151,535
2.1% growth/year

* Indexed Annuity with downside protection and 5% cap
** Average investor returns 1992-2011, Dalbar study
Excludes trading costs, fees and taxes.

Distribution (Retirement Income Years)

Flash forward, to carry the same two examples into the distribution years. The first possibility, of course, is that Joe wants to cash out of his accounts and do something else with the money. He has this option in both cases – market-based accounts or annuity. For the purposes of this book, however, lifetime income is the goal. So, we'll assume that Joe converts his accounts into retirement income at age 60. Continuing with average investor scenario, imagine that Joe begins to withdraw $6,100 annually (about 4%) from his $151,536 non-guaranteed market-based nest egg – adjusting by 3% per year for inflation. For the sake of simplicity, we'll assume that what's left in his portfolio continues to earn 2.1% per year – although, in reality, market volatility can have a big impact on distributions from accounts containing securities.

Figure 13

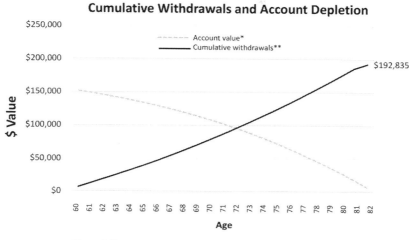

**Market-based Account
Cumulative Withdrawals and Account Depletion**

*Assumes 2.1% average annual return based on Dalbar's study (1992-2011)
**Assumes an initial withdrawal of $6100 adjusted for 3% inflation annually
Excludes trading costs, fees, and taxes

Figure 13 shows a snapshot of his account depletion and cumulative income as he takes systematic withdrawals over the years. At this pace, Joe will run out of money when he is 82 – after withdrawing a total of $192,835 over the years. If he lives longer than 82, he will need to rely on other sources of funds for income.

Next, take a look at the annuity scenario during the distribution stage. Imagine that Joe decides to turn his $204,087 annuity into lifetime income. Using the example payout structure shared in a prior chapter (Figure 8) to estimate, Joe would receive annual payments of $10,204 for life (assuming 5% for a single annuitant), whether he lives to be 82 or 102 – *even if* there is no money left in his accumulation account. That is the value of insurance.

Let's say that Joe lives to be 100 as shown in Figure 14. He would receive $418,364 in income payments over the years – even though his cash accumulation account would have been depleted years earlier. Of course, if he passed away while value remained in his cash accumulation account, his heirs would get what's left.

Figure 14

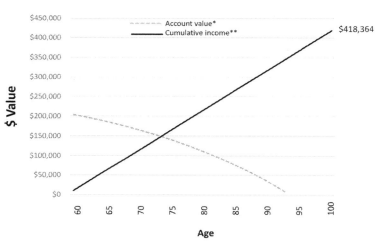

Annuity: Cumulative Income and Cash Account Depletion

*Assumes fixed indexed annuity (5% cap) cash account grows at 3.6% average annual return
**Assumes a 5% payout for a single annuitant, at $10,204 per year
Excludes trading costs, fees, and taxes

These examples take two contrasting return profiles all the way from accumulation through distribution. However, you may be bothered by using different rates of return during distribution. So, let's balance the playing field and imagine that we start with the same dollar amount ($200,000) at the end of accumulation and that our non-guaranteed market account and annuity earn exactly the same rate during the distribution years. Assuming that the annuity's payout percentage is 5%, Joe's annual income payment will be $10,000. We'll assume that he takes the same amount from his market-based account as well.

Figure 15

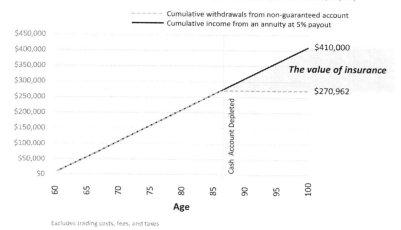

Cumulative Income Distribution
Annuity Vs Non-Guaranteed Account
($200,000 account values at start, 2.5% growth rate, $10,000 distribution per year)

At this pace, Joe's non-guaranteed market account will run out of cash early in his 87th year after collecting $270,962 in payments. His annuity, on the other hand, will continue to pay him for life. If he lives to 100, the annuity would put $410,000 dollars in his pocket over time – $139,038 more than the non-guaranteed account.

This is the value of insurance. In this example, which option do *you* think would have provided the better return?

Before leaving this topic, I would like to acknowledge this: Market indexes are useful as directional indicators. Financial advisors (including me) use them all the time to test scenarios and demonstrate patterns. That is different from buying into an index as a realistic personal target – which it is not.

> ### A Case from Real Life
>
> *Steve and Carolyn are a busy couple in their late-forties with two active teenagers. They had been disciplined savers and had built a portfolio invested primarily in mutual funds and individual stocks. While gazing at his statements one day, Steve noticed some fine print that summarized the returns on one large fund at 0.5% -- far from the 8% average return touted in the brochure. Shocked by the result for this particular fund, he decided to analyze the portfolio's overall performance through the years. What he found was demoralizing: his money had been growing at a pace of about 2.6% per year. He had expected much more. "We are so busy with work, soccer practice, dance classes, and life, that we don't have the time or inclination to watch the market." Hoping to retire at 60, Steve and Carolyn focused on safe money – shifting part of their portfolio to a indexed annuity with a 5% cap and an income rider. As Steve put it, "The return might not impress Wall Street, but it adds a safety net to our portfolio. And, more importantly, I can see real value in securing income for life."*

The Myth of Average Returns

"The naive believes everything, but the sensible man considers his steps."
Proverbs 14:15

There's no sense challenging the false lure of a market index without taking on a sister temptation of average rate of return.

Average Vs. Annualized Return

When mutual fund companies promote their historical returns, they generally reference the *simple average* rate of return, rather than the return an investor actually receives – called the *annualized return* or compound annual growth rate (CAGR). A broker might say, for instance, a particular fund has *averaged* 13% return over the last 5 years. This practice is so universal that no one gives it a second thought.

The primary issue with this routine is that an *average* rate of return is misleading. If you had an investment that went up 100% one year and fell by 50% the next, your average return would be 25%. But who cares? Your principal would be back to its starting point, so your real annualized gain would be 0%. In this example, 25% is the simple average (not meaningful from an investment perspective), and 0% is the **annualized return** or Compound Annual Growth Rate (**CAGR**) that you *actually* earned.

CAGR is always smaller. Statistically, there's a 1-2% difference between the average returns that the media and mutual fund companies promote and what you realize as your true annualized return.

The Dalbar study from the last chapter provides a useful comparative example: Over the twenty year period ending Dec. 31, 2011, the stock market's true *annualized return*, or CAGR, was 7.8%. The *average* return was 9.6%. (And despite both of these stellar benchmarks, in reality the average investor only earned 2.1%).

If you want to explore historical differences between average and annualized returns, check out Money Chimp's Compound Annual Growth Rate (CAGR) Calculator.[29] You can enter a date range and see for yourself. You can even adjust for inflation.

Rosy but Misleading

To understand how the promise of average returns can present a rosier picture than reality, consider the hypothetical market shown in Figure 16, with growth rates oscillating between +10% and -10%

each year for 10 years. In this text book illustration, the **average return** is 0%.

[(5 years x 10%) + (5 years x -10%)] / 10 years = 0%

Conventional wisdom would have you believe that if you buy and hold, your portfolio will weather those ups and downs. At 0% average return, you won't gain, but you shouldn't lose. Right?

Figure 16

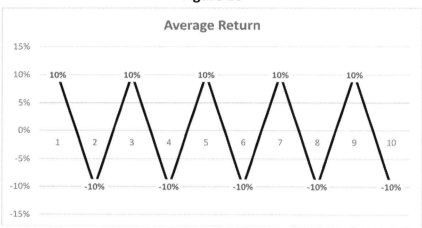

Wrong. If you were to put $1,000 into this hypothetical market and hold for 10 years, Figure 17 shows the result: You would *lose* $49, for a *negative* **actual rate of return.** Ouch!

While the real market would never show such a uniform pattern, the math is true for whatever up and down movements occur. If the market ever has a negative day (and we know that it does), it is mathematically impossible to achieve the average rate of return.

Of course, it's not the average return per se that is most troublesome – it's all of those downturns that wreak havoc on your future income. Because, when you experience a loss, the sad truth is that it takes time to make it up.

Figure 17

| Year | Normal Exposure to Down Cycles | |
	Average Return	Value of $1000
Start		$ 1,000
1	10%	$ 1,100
2	-10%	$ 990
3	10%	$ 1,089
4	-10%	$ 980
5	10%	$ 1,078
6	-10%	$ 970
7	10%	$ 1,067
8	-10%	$ 961
9	10%	$ 1,057
10	-10%	$ 951

The Benefit of Downside Protection

What if you could gain during the up cycles and stay whole during the down cycles? By now you know that you can. An **indexed annuity** provides a mechanism. The growth of your funds in an indexed annuity is tied to market gains. If the stock market goes up, you keep a certain percentage of that gain. If the stock market goes down, an indexed annuity has downside protection, meaning that your account will not lose value when the market has a negative return. You don't lose a penny — even if the market takes a bone-chilling hit. Imagine how pleased the owner of an indexed annuity would have been with downside protection in 2001 when the market gave up 12% of its value, followed by a 22% decline in 2002. Or, in 2008, when the market tanked 37%.

For a side by side comparison of a volatile market investment versus an indexed annuity, let's plug some dollars and cents into the theoretical market we considered in Figures 16-17. In this mathematical demonstration, we'll start with the same $1,000. On the left, we'll imagine investing in the sample market. On the right, we'll imagine investing in an indexed annuity with a 5% cap. The example market will still vacillate between +10% and -10% return for 10 years.

The scenario on the left benefits from the full market gain, but suffers during the down cycles. The indexed annuity, on the right, participates in the upside (with a 5% cap) and gets full protection during the downside. Notice how the **annuity locks in gains**. The base account value (or "basis" in industry lingo) **resets at the higher value** achieved during the rise and *sticks* until the market starts going up again. When the market goes up, your value builds from a high achieved during the earlier up cycle. When the market goes down, nothing happens to *your* money. Your value is insured against losses.

Figure 18

Year	Normal Exposure to Down Cycles		Downside Protection		
	Market Return	Value of $1000	Indexed Annuity, 5% cap	Value	
Start		$ 1,000		$ 1,000	
1	10%	$ 1,100	5%	$ 1,050	*Locked in gains*
2	-10%	$ 990		$ 1,050	Downside protection
3	10%	$ 1,089	5%	$ 1,103	*Locked in gains*
4	-10%	$ 980		$ 1,103	Downside protection
5	10%	$ 1,078	5%	$ 1,158	*Locked in gains*
6	-10%	$ 970		$ 1,158	Downside protection
7	10%	$ 1,067	5%	$ 1,216	*Locked in gains*
8	-10%	$ 961		$ 1,216	Downside protection
9	10%	$ 1,057	5%	$ 1,276	*Locked in gains*
10	-10%	$ 951		$ 1,276	Downside protection

Meanwhile, the investment on the left loses ground. Look at the difference in account values in the identical up and down market. At the end of this imaginary 10-year game, our original $1000 would have either grown by \$276 in the indexed annuity, or it would have lost \$49 in the market. In volatile markets, it is hard to argue with the kind of protection an indexed annuity can offer.

When Buy and Hold Breaks Down

"Money is better than poverty, if only for financial reasons." Woody Allen

Buy and hold is somewhat of a mantra in the investing world. It's generally good advice during the accumulation years, when time is on your side. It's designed to prevent panic selling – one of the irrational behaviors that destroys portfolio value.

Recovery Takes Time

The buy and hold strategy is predicated on the notion that average returns will work in our favor over the long run and the market will bounce back — *quick enough.* But what if it doesn't? Take a look at the historical recap of market crashes below[30]. You might be surprised by the amount of time it takes the market to recover.

Figure 19: The Worse U.S. Market Crashes

Dates	Percent Decline	Days Duration (Market Top to Bottom)	Total Recovery Time (to get back to even)
1901-1903	46.1%	875	2 years
1906-1907	48.5%	665	9 years
1916-1917	40.1%	393	2 years
1919-1921	46.6%	669	3 years
1930-1932	86.0%	813	22 years
1939-1942	40.4%	959	3 years
1973-1974	45.1%	694	8 years
2000-2002	37.8%	999	4 years
2007-2009	50.9%	429	2 years

Wall Street is not alone in this global economy of ours. In 1989,

Japan's Nikkei average hit an all-time high of 38,957 having grown six-fold in the prior decade[31]. By 2009, it had lost nearly all of these gains, closing at 7,054.98 on March 10, 2009—81.9% below its peak twenty years earlier. At the time of this writing, the Nikkei was hovering around 19,883, still far below its peak more than a quarter of a century ago.

Timing is Everything

"Well, they call you lady luck, but there is room for doubt. At times you have a very un-lady-like way of running out." Frank Sinatra, Luck Be a Lady

The good news is that markets recover. The bad news is that it can take time. Most people understand that risk tolerance goes down as we age, because we have less time to recover. However, you may not know that the risks of losses are more severe in retirement, when we are withdrawing money, than they are during the accumulation years when we are depositing money.

I would bet my bottom dollar that you're familiar with the notion of buy and hold, however, I doubt that you have ever heard the *sequence of returns* mentioned. Yet, sequence **could be the most important factor in determining how long your money will last!**

During the accumulation stage of your financial life, the order of positive and negative returns seems to be of little consequence. Dollars invested over time average out, and few people give it a second thought. But throw in a distribution, and your attitude will inevitably change. In this case, the sequence of returns can make a substantial difference. Returns during **the earliest years of your retirement will define your later years**. If you're caught on the wrong end of a cycle during the early years of retirement, the effect on your income can be devastating.

Simply put, if you retire into a down cycle first (like many did in 2001, 2002, or 2008), you will run out of money much sooner than if you were to experience positive returns first — even at the same average return over the course of your retirement. Distributions exacerbate the losses. Plus, it takes much larger returns to recover what you lost. Since we don't control the market, and we have limited control over the timing of our retirement, this *luck of the draw* can pose a significant obstacle to an income plan.

The two scenarios in Figure 20 illustrate the impact of sequence of returns. Both use the returns from 1992 to 2011[20] — which is a snapshot you have seen before in Dalbar's study. You already know that the annualized return was 7.82% during this time.

Imagine that Joe Investor retired at age 63, with a $500,000 nest egg. Joe started with a 4% or $20,000 distribution in his first year and adjusted by 3% each year for inflation.

Figure 20: Impact of Sequence of Returns

	Positive Years Early					Negative Years Early		
Year	Stock Market Return	Withdrawal at Start of Year	Nest Egg at Start of Year	Age	Year	Stock Market Return	Withdrawal at Start of Year	Nest Egg at Start of Year
1992	7.60%	$20,000	$500,000	63	1	-37.22%	$20,000	$500,000
1993	10.17%	$20,600	$516,480	64	2	7.60%	$20,600	$301,344
1994	1.19%	$21,218	$546,311	65	3	-11.98%	$21,218	$302,081
1995	38.02%	$21,855	$531,342	66	4	-9.11%	$21,855	$247,215
1996	23.06%	$22,510	$703,194	67	5	23.06%	$22,510	$204,830
1997	33.67%	$23,185	$837,650	68	6	10.82%	$23,185	$224,363
1998	28.73%	$23,881	$1,088,694	69	7	4.79%	$23,881	$222,945
1999	21.11%	$24,597	$1,370,734	70	8	5.46%	$24,597	$208,599
2000	-9.11%	$25,335	$1,630,306	71	9	-22.27%	$25,335	$194,048
2001	-11.98%	$26,095	$1,458,758	72	10	28.72%	$26,095	$131,140
2002	-22.27%	$26,878	$1,261,029	73	11	2.07%	$26,878	$135,214
2003	28.72%	$27,685	$959,305	74	12	14.87%	$27,685	$110,578
2004	10.82%	$28,515	$1,199,182	75	13	15.74%	$28,515	$95,220
2005	4.79%	$29,371	$1,297,333	76	14	33.67%	$29,371	$77,204
2006	15.74%	$30,252	$1,328,698	77	15	1.19%	$30,252	$63,939
2007	5.46%	$31,159	$1,502,822	78	16	27.11%	$31,159	$34,088
2008	-37.22%	$32,094	$1,552,015	79	17	10.17%	$3,722	$3,722
2009	27.11%	$33,057	$954,206	80	18	28.73%	$0	$0
2010	14.87%	$34,049	$1,170,873	81	19	21.11%	$0	$0
2011	2.07%	$35,070	$1,305,870	82	20	38.02%	$0	$0

Total Withdrawals: $537,407   Total Withdrawals: $406,860

The columns on the left shows how this plan would have played out if Joe had retired in 1992 and followed the market until 2011. As luck would have it, returns were strong in the beginning of this time capsule. He would have enjoyed eight years of positive returns (1992-1999) before the first negative year in 2000. Joe would have easily kept up his annual paychecks as planned, withdrawing $537,407 over the years with money to spare at age 82. Joe's golden years would have had a golden start!

But what if fate had blown the other way? The scenario on the right uses exactly the same set of returns, but scrambles the order so that the negative years hit Joe straight out of the shoot. Everything else is the same: $500,000 nest egg with an initial withdrawal of $20,000 adjusted by 3% per year for inflation. The example market still offers a 7.82% annualized return during the 20-year journey. The only difference is the *sequence of returns*. Joe suffers from negative returns in the beginning and, in this case, runs out of money in 17 years after withdrawing only $406,860 —a full 24% less at age 82 than in the prior example where he benefited from positive returns in earlier years. In the second case, the losses from the early negative years were compounded by the distribution, and Joe's portfolio never caught up. Lady Luck wasn't with him.

Insure Your Income

When you consider possible swings of luck, you can see the **value that annuities can provide.** The objective is to meet your retirement income goals *even if* the sequence of returns falls on the wrong side of luck in the early years of your retirement.

In the example above, a fixed indexed annuity would have mitigated the risk of market losses early in Joe's retirement years and locked in gains during the up years. But, more importantly, a

guaranteed paycheck for life would have been the real boon for Joe. One look at the right-hand columns in Figure 20 show how much Joe would have appreciated a guaranteed income stream around year 17 when his account ran dry.

A Case from Real Life

Robert and Jackie clinked their glasses in a toast. They had informed their employers that they would retire in six months. It was a day they had anticipated for many years – looking forward to travel, golfing, family time, hobbies, and a condo on the coast.

They had enjoyed playing the stock market, and it had paid off. It was mid-October 2007, and the market was sizzling. The S&P 500 had hit an all-time high of 1565.15 on October 7th, and their portfolio was worth $2.3 million. The timing seemed right.

On April 11, 2008, Robert and Jackie said good-bye to the work world and hello to retirement. Some of the elation they felt in October was dampened, because their portfolio value had dropped to $1.96 million. But, they reminded each other that they had weathered market storms before and that it would bounce back. They could live on the money in their bank account for a few months while they waited for an up-tick.

On September 29, 2008, they had a rocky day. The S&P 500 had plunged nearly 10% and closed at 1106.42. Their portfolio was now worth $1.6 million and they hadn't withdrawn a dime! That was $700,000 less than they had when they decided to retire – the equivalent of several years of work.

On October 10, 2008, they could wait no longer. They had to begin withdrawals from their securities-based accounts to cover living expenses. With the S&P 500 at 899.22, their portfolio was worth $1.3

---

*million (a cool million under their original high). Following the 4%
rule, they would withdraw $52,894 per year – a far cry from the
$92,000 retirement income they had expected one year earlier. Sadly,
the decline wasn't over. The S&P 500 hit a 11 ½ year low of 752.44 on
November 20, 2008 – taking Jackie and Robert's account values to
$1.1 million. Some of their big plans would have to wait.*

*NOTE: These are real numbers. The S&P 500 fell by more than 50%
between October 7, 2007 and November 20, 2008. For Robert and
Jackie, the timing was bad and the result devastating. At ages 62 and
65, they were unlikely to replace this income. They had followed the
buy and hold rule and maintained a risk-tolerant position because it
had worked in the past. They hadn't anticipated the impact that the
sequence of returns could have in the early years of their retirement.*

Inflation: The Income Eater

Planning your future income is clearly tied to your assumptions
about returns. Equally important are your assumptions about
inflation and how it will impact the future value of your money. If
recent history is any indicator, the value of a dollar will continue to
decline. You will need more dollars in the future simply to maintain
today's standard of living. I doubt that is news to you. The big
question is how much of your retirement savings and spending
power will be eaten by inflation.

If inflation averages 3% for the next 20 years (the most common
assumption), a dollar in the year 2016 will be worth 54¢ in 2036,
meaning you will need to save $90,306 to be able to buy the same
amount $50,000 will buy today. Of course, the challenge isn't the
math, the challenge is the assumption. Even the most revered world
economists haven't been able to predict the inflation rate with any

accuracy. Will inflation will average 3% over the next few decades? According to the U.S. Inflation Calculator[32], the inflation rate averaged 2.3% over the past 20 years (1996-2015), and 5.6% in the 1980s. What the future holds is every economist's best guess.

Since the main job of an annuity is to mitigate future income risk, as you might imagine, many annuities offer riders that address inflationary pressures by providing annual income adjustments. Like any rider, this is an option you may want to explore with your financial advisor.

The Risk of Cognitive Decline

"Old age ain't for sissies, honey." Bette Davis

Market risks aren't the only perils we face in retirement – health ranks high on the list as well. Although it may be hard to imagine in the prime of our lives, statistics show that there is a fairly high risk of cognitive decline as we grow older. In 2007, Harvard economist David Laibson published a study showing the effects of age on the quality of financial decision making (*The Age of Reason: Financial Decisions Over the Lifecycle*)[33]. He showed that financial decisions made by older adults are weaker than middle-aged adults. The elderly consistently pay higher interest rates and fees, and are often victims of financial fraud. Sadly, reduced cognitive ability is partly to blame.

In his 2014 article *Use Annuities to Protect Yourself From Yourself*, Jeffrey Brown (Economics PhD from MIT and Associate Director of the Retirement Research Center at the National Bureau of Economic Research)[34] points to annuities as a strong strategy for mitigating the risk of cognitive decline and the impact it could have on your future financial health.

As you already know, annuities address longevity risk by providing a predictable monthly income for life – guaranteeing that you will not outlive your money. By extension, they provide another subtle benefit as well: they ensure your ability to meet your basic needs even if you make a few questionable money decisions in the future. As Brown puts it, "Even in the event that a fraudster tries to bilk you out of your savings, you will always have a steady paycheck coming in each month on which to live."

Misconceptions about Annuities

"To often we enjoy the comfort of opinion, without the discomfort of thought." John F. Kennedy

Finally, let's slay the dragon of misconceptions. If you have been researching annuities for any time at all, you have undoubtedly noticed that people either love them or hate them. Why they are the topic of so much heated debate is a complete enigma. After all, the work is the same whether you are evaluating an annuity or some other potential investment (e.g., stocks, bonds, mutual funds, real estate, life insurance, etc.). Either way, you have to assess the options – given your own personal set of objectives, financial realities, and risk tolerance – to decide what's appropriate and what's not. Nevertheless, opinions about annuities abound, both schooled and unschooled.

I once overheard a stock broker describing the perils of annuities to some friends. Many of his points were wrong, exaggerated, or outdated. Either he was unlicensed to sell annuities and, therefore, unschooled, or he was a poor student. Regardless, I felt sorry for his audience. It made me realize how much misinformation is out there (often perpetuated by someone in a competitive field). So, I would like to take this opportunity to hit four common misconceptions head on.

Misconception #1: Loss of control

"Life is difficult and complicated and beyond anyone's total control, and the humility to know that will enable you to survive its vicissitudes." J.K. Rowling

Control. Ah, control. I can practically feel your jaw clamping down on the word as I write. Most of us like to feel we are in control on some level. We want to control our health, wealth, family, future, possessions, etc. But, deep down, we know we can't control what J.K. Rowling calls "life's vicissitudes." Life is unpredictable. We can eat right and exercise, and be hit by a bus tomorrow. We can build an idyllic house on the coast, and be wiped out by a hurricane a week later. We can make all the right investment decisions during our working years, and watch our nest egg dwindle in a down market moments before retirement. The point is, **control is an illusion**.

Nevertheless, one common objection to annuities is the fear of losing control. I have always been mystified by this. It seems to me that one has less control over money exposed to the volatile market without any sort of safety net. But, let's go with the fear and explore a few pillars of control. When I ask people what they mean by "control," this is what they say they want: (1) control over returns, and (2) access to their money. Let's dig into both desires a little more thoughtfully.

Control Over Returns

Stockbrokers will generally tell you that putting your money into an annuity for lifetime income means that you will lose control over your returns and principal. (I know it's cynical, but I think this actually means that the *stockbroker* would prefer to control your principal.) However, think back on almost every example we have looked at so far for a dose of reality regarding control over returns.

- Dalbar studies have shown time and again that average investors lag market returns by a mile for many reasons. If your hope is to match market rates of return, check your assumptions. Control doesn't necessarily mean success.

- Because markets have negative years (and you don't control this), it's mathematically impossible for investors to earn the average rates of returns touted in the market. Eliminate the down cycles? Voila! Better results. If you want to control your principal and gains, the best bet is to insulate yourself from the down cycles with an annuity.

- In the early years of your retirement, Lady Luck will determine your future by dealing a set of cards with either positive or negative returns. The sequence of returns is beyond your control, but is probably the biggest contributor to how long your money will last during retirement. The best way to control this risk is to protect your money from negative returns while keeping the gains achieved during the good years.

If the goal is a guaranteed paycheck for life, then the kind of control the stock broker touts is an illusion.

Liquidity and Access

Accessibility (liquidity) is best examined under the light of comparisons. Remember, brokers make money when money moves. Good for them; not necessarily good for you. Nevertheless, there are times when *you* need access. So, consider how accessible your funds would be if invested in any of the following vehicles.

- **Bank Savings Account:** This is the ultimate in accessibility. You can have your money any time. You will earn substantially less than inflation and pay monthly fees for common courtesies like paper statements — meaning that you lose ground every day. Accessible, but costly.

- **Certificate of Deposit:** In exchange for a slightly better interest rate, you can lock your funds in a CD for a period of time. The longer you lock up your funds, the better the interest rate. While the rates are nothing to write home about, it beats the savings account. If you decide to withdraw your money sooner than the agreed term, you'll pay a penalty. So, your money is somewhat accessible, but not without a cost.

- **Bonds:** High quality bonds are generally a safe investment with predictably lower returns. If there is a ready market, you can get in and out when you want to. That doesn't mean that losses are impossible. When interest rates go up, bond prices fall. Nevertheless, bonds rank relatively high on the accessibility scale. You can get to your money for better or worse.

- **Mutual Funds:** By combining the money of many investors into a single, professionally managed bag of stocks, bonds and other funds, mutual funds spread volatility risk better than you could accomplish on your own. Nevertheless, the money is in the market. Therefore, most mutual funds follow the market up and down. You can pull your money out at any time, assuming the risk that the value could be higher or lower than where you started. While there are some no-risk mutual funds invested in government T-bills that don't lose money, they don't gain much either.

- **Stocks:** You can move money in and out of the stock market any time. However, the decision to take it out is a matter of timing. If you invest $1,000 and the market steals half of it, you're stuck. Toss a coin: buy and hold until your portfolio recovers (remember that could take a while), or sell and lose. Accessible? Yes. But, accessibility is married to Lady Luck.

- **Real Estate:** If you have a taste for real estate, it probably means that you're chasing cash flow and/or appreciation. Cash flow is dependent on having reliable tenants and keeping expenses low. Real appreciation depends on market conditions beyond your control. Either way, if you want to pull your money out of real estate, it won't be quick, so it ranks low on the accessibility scale. And, again, if you purchased a $250,000 house and the real estate market tanks? Buy and hold, or sell and lose. Accessible? No.

The liquidity of an annuity depends on what type of annuity you buy, what options you select, and whether you are in the accumulation or distribution stage. Annuities are long-term investments. No question. You agree to put your money into an annuity for a certain period of time. During the accumulation years, most policies allow you to withdraw 10% per year without penalty. If you withdraw more than that before the time expires, you will pay surrender fees. Admittedly, annuities have limited liquidity at this stage. When you reach the distribution stage, however, you can do whatever you want to do with your money. You can withdraw it completely, turn it into lifetime income with an income rider (which allows you control over your principal), or turn it into lifetime income by annuitizing (the only choice where you relinquish control).

If liquidity during the early years is your primary concern, then an annuity probably isn't for you. If liquidity during retirement is your goal, then annuities provide ample opportunity.

Misconception #2: Poor returns

The second misconception is that annuities are "bad investments" – meaning that you can make more money elsewhere. Investors and financial advisors are conditioned to focus exclusively on Internal Rate of Return (IRR) or Return on Investment (ROI). For most investments, this perspective is fine because the duration and dollars generated are clear.

But, what if these two data elements are unknown? Sure, an annuity delivers a particular growth rate during a predefined accumulation period, but it also provides an additional return of lifetime income payments. The cumulative value of these payments will depend on when the annuitant activates payments and how long he or she lives – both unknowns. This makes it challenging to find apples-to-apples comparisons for annuities. It can be difficult to compare asset classes when one is guaranteed and the other is not. An asset providing a guarantee provides an advantage to the buyer that the other one lacks, but placing a specific value on this feature depends on a host of assumptions.

Cash value provides another conceptual hurdle. Traditional advisors often focus on the cash value of the annuity – diminishing the value of guarantees. Yet, one of the primary reasons for buying an annuity is the income guarantee it offers. In that sense, the cash value is secondary to the guarantees. As you know by now, income riders can offer an additional income benefit beyond the return an investor sees in his or her cash accumulation account. This gives the investor a "back-up" plan that other investments cannot provide.

If you want to compare annuities with other types of investments, page back to prior discussion topics. You have seen how the tax deferred growth and guaranteed income streams of annuities can top the returns generated by other safe money options, like CDs and Bonds (See figures 2 and 10). You also know that most investors are unlikely beat a market index or achieve the average return. If you are using one of those indicators as your target, remember to temper your expectations appropriately. The average investor usually falls 70% below the market promise.[35]

All that said, the real value of annuities is in their contractual guarantees more than pure growth. As you may recall, the best way to understand the return profile of an annuity is to break your investigation into two stages – accumulation and distribution. Each stage offers bang for your buck. See Figures 13-15 for a reminder of how it works.

Misconception #3: Higher fees

Misconceptions about fees sometimes discourage people from considering an annuity as an important addition to their portfolio. I doubt anyone expects a free lunch, but are annuities actually more costly than the alternatives? Let's take a look at the fee structure for annuities. Then, we'll examine how they stack up against the alternatives.

Naturally, before making any investment choice, you need to know the lay of the land. The more you know, the better prepared you are to ask meaningful questions. Clearly understanding the features, related costs, and benefits will help you assess whether annuities match your objectives. Types of fees vary according to the types of annuities and features you select. So, start with the big picture:

- Be clear about your objectives.
- Identify the type of annuity most suited to your needs.
- Understand basic costs – free of bells and whistles.

- Explore the costs and benefits of extra features that interest you.

Like many products you are accustomed to buying, **extra features cost money**. A car with a bigger engine, leather seats, and premium tires costs more than the basic brand. The same is true for annuities. Since the cost of extra features can take a bite out of your overall return, you should only choose what you expect to use. Take time to research how each feature works, including costs and benefits, then determine which riders (if any) suit your specific needs.

Focus on understanding value over the entire life cycle of your investment – during both accumulation and distribution. While the value equation may focus on returns during accumulation; payout and lifetime guarantees add value during distribution. Evaluate the guarantees and features the annuity promises, along with any related restrictions or boundaries, versus the cost of those features.

When comparing products, remember that part of what you are paying for is **the strength of the insurance company** standing behind the guarantees. For example, a higher payout rate offered by an insurance company with questionable financial strength is not attractive. See the earlier section in this book called "Are Annuity Companies Safe?" for guidelines on assessing the creditworthiness of a carrier.

Knowledge is power, so find the best teachers that you can. Seek out advisors who are experts in the annuity world. In order to sell annuities of any kind, an advisor must be licensed to sell insurance. To sell variable annuities, they must also have a securities license. All too often, investors ask their stock brokers about annuities without realizing that he or she may not be licensed or properly informed. Fees vary from product to product, so read about any investment you're considering – whether annuities or otherwise.

Annuity companies have to list and explain the various costs of ownership in the annuity prospectus (for variable annuities) or statement of understanding (for fixed annuities).

Types of Annuity Fees

Annuity companies cover their expenses and profit with some combination of the following:

1. **Investment management fees.** Applicable to variable annuities only, these are management fees related to the underlying investments (stocks, bonds, funds, money market instruments and related assets). Check out the prospectus to investigate likely management fees.

2. **Mortality and expense (M&E) / Administrative**. Also pertaining only to variable annuities, these charges cover insurance costs for guarantees, selling, and administrative expenses.

3. **Surrender charges**. Most annuities limit the amount of money you can withdraw from your account during the initial years of a contract. If you withdraw more than that limit during that predefined period, you will pay a surrender fee. Surrender charges – which can be substantial – typically decrease with time, so the longer you hold your annuity, the lower the surrender charge will be. For example, one common surrender fee is 7% of the annuity's value if the money is withdrawn during the first year. The penalty drops one percent per year until there is no penalty after the seventh year. Insurance companies temper the blow by providing measured liquidity during this time, generally allowing investors to withdraw up to 10% per year without a penalty. Be sure to understand the ins and outs to ensure that you have the kind of flexibility you

need.

4. **Rider charges.** If you opt for riders offering additional features (e.g., income, cost of living, death benefits, etc.), you may pay an additional fee.

5. **Conservative returns or payouts.** Some annuities (e.g., fixed, indexed, or immediate) have fewer explicit fees, opting instead to recoup their costs and profits by offering more conservative returns or payouts. During accumulation, insurance companies earn their keep in the spread between what they pay you and what they can earn in the market. Fixed annuities offer conservative fixed interest rates, while indexed annuities cap your participation in market growth. During the distribution years, the insurance company defines a payout percentage which allows them to cover their costs. As emphasized in an earlier chapter, pay keen attention to the payout rate for any annuity, as this determines the size of your future paycheck.

The fee structure depends on the type of annuity you buy – variable, fixed, or indexed – and whether it's deferred or immediate. Variable annuities generally have explicit fees, while fixed and indexed annuities are more likely to cover their costs by offering more conservative returns or payouts. Nearly all annuities have surrender charges and fees for optional features (riders). Figure 21 summarizes the types of fees you might expect to see for each type of annuity.

Figure 21: Types of Annuity Fees

Type of Fee	Variable	Fixed	Indexed
M&E, Administrative	Yes	No	No
Management fees for underlying investments	Yes	No	No
Surrender charges	Yes	Yes	Yes
Optional Riders / Features	Optional	Optional	Optional
Flat contract fees	Yes	No	No
Conservative returns or payout rates	+/- Per Market	Yes	Yes

Fixed annuities offer a guaranteed interest rate for a set period of time. The interest rate is conservative enough to pay for the insurance company's expenses and profits, so you generally will not see other fees unless you (a) elect to purchase optional riders or (b) withdraw more than the agreed amount before the surrender period expires, thereby activating surrender charges. Because the rates and periods are clearly stated in the contract, it is easy to compare fixed annuities with other similar products. Pay as much attention to the guarantee period as you do to the rate. Look for products that guarantee interest rates at least as long as the surrender fees are applicable.

Indexed annuities promise upside potential based on the performance of a stock or bond market index. You will generally pay fewer fees, however, the insurance company makes up the difference by capping your participation in market increases. In this way their expenses and profits are embedded in your return. When comparing indexed annuities, ask about the annual cap which defines how much your annuity can actually earn.

Variable annuities include M&E / administrative fees,

management fees for the underlying investments, and fees for optional features – all of which can impact your initial payout amount. When looking at variable products, compare the features, fees and payout structure – with an eye for the *total* costs. You may find that one variable annuity charges a lower mortality and expense fee, but higher administrative fees and feature costs, making the entire package more costly than the next. Variable annuities have a reputation for being relatively high cost, because they come with management fees for the mutual funds in their sub-accounts, plus administration and mortality fees from the insurance company. In total, the fees for variable annuities can top 3-4% per year. The value equation works for many investors. It is up to you to determine whether the benefits justify the costs – like you would for any investment.

Single premium immediate annuities (SPIA) have no annual fees, but the insurance company gains by limiting liquidity. In this way, the expenses are built in to the payout structure. It's easy to compare prices for immediate annuities, as you can focus on the payout.

For an additional fee, most annuities allow you to add features (e.g., lifetime income guarantees, cost of living adjustments, death benefits, etc.). Depending on the additional riders you elect to attach to the policy, optional fees can range from 0.5% to 1.5% on average.

Beyond explicit fees, investors want to understand hidden costs like commissions, opportunity costs, and tax. Obviously, **commissions** (or similar means of compensation) are not unique to annuities. This is a common practice in the finance world. In the case of annuities, however, commissions are paid directly from the insurance company to the advisor, so you will never actually see these costs come out of your premium. If you deposit $100,000 into an annuity, the entire $100,000 will be applied to your policy and begin to earn money. Nevertheless, commissions are part of the costs of doing business for the insurance company, so the company will recoup the cost somewhere – generally through one of the five mechanisms described above. **Opportunity cost** is the cost of tying up your money. That means you could miss opportunities to put your money elsewhere when markets are booming. Any financial vehicle that ties your money up for a period of time has opportunity cost – whether it's tied up in an annuity with surrender chargers, in a depressed stock market, or in real estate. Regarding **taxes**, annuities benefit from tax-deferred growth, but when you take the money out, you'll pay taxes. As the saying goes, "There are only two certainties in life – death and taxes." Taxes are a pay-me-now or pay-me-later proposition depending on the investments you choose to make.

While fees are an inevitable irritation no matter what investment platform you choose, here's a pleasant surprise you will find only in the annuity world. **A bonus!** Many annuities actually offer a deposit bonus. For example, if an investor puts $100,000 into an annuity paying a 4% bonus, the insurance company will add $4,000 to the income account. That's an extra chunk of change that realizes positive growth from day one. Perhaps this one should be called an "anti-fee."

Are Annuities Out of Line?

Given this background, are annuities out of line when compared to other investment options? Let's take a look at mutual funds. In a 2011 article[36] titled *The Real Cost of Owning a Mutual Fund*, Forbes broke down the cost components of owning a mutual fund. When you consider the expense ratios at 0.9% per year, plus transaction costs (commissions, market impact, and spread) at 1.44% per year, plus cash drag (the cost of liquidity) at 0.83% per year, plus tax cost ratio for taxable accounts at 1.0-1.2% per year –**a mutual fund can cost you 3.17-4.37% per year.** You have to make a hefty return to make that up each year.

Some financial advisors and wealth managers provide fee structures based on the size of your account – ranging from **1.0%** to **3.0%** – year after year **for the duration of the account.**[37] Annual flat fees, costing thousands of dollars per year, are another possibility. These fees come directly out of the client's investment capital thereby reducing the amount available for growth. In contrast, annuity commissions are paid out of the insurance carrier's general fund (never from the annuity buyer's premium). They are paid once versus annually and capped based on the deposit amount. This protects the client's core investment for growth.

It's impossible to recap costs across all asset classes industry wide. Suffice it to say that financial services and products of any type cost money. And the fees and commission structures vary as much as the products themselves. Regardless of which asset class, product, and provider you consider, you must take the time to understand fees and expenses, and to do your own cost-benefit analysis.

Misconception #4: Unfavorable Legislation

I'm mystified by this misconception – since I only see benefits in recent legislation – however, I have heard this statement repeated by financial advisors outside of the annuities market more than once. So, let's address it. There's no need for legislation to weigh heavily on your mind.

There are two areas of recent legislative activity impacting the annuities market. In both cases, the objective is safety for investors.

- In 2014, the IRS approved qualified longevity annuity contracts, or QLACs, for use in traditional IRAs, 401(k)s, 403(b)s, and some other retirement plans. This legislation directs a portion of your retirement account to be used as an annuity in your later years to guarantee income.

- The U.S. Department of Labor recently passed heightened fiduciary duties for anyone giving retirement advice.[38] This legislation offers a broader definition of fiduciary responsibility which benefits investors in two ways: (1) advisors will continue to enrich their skills and business practices or be eliminated from the playing field, and (2) providers will continue to improve their products.

The idea that annuities will somehow become unavailable is ludicrous. Annuities have been around since Caesar. That's a good indicator that they are here to stay.

Of course, tax laws change all the time. For example, in 2003, George W. Bush signed a new set of tax cuts into law which clipped capital gains taxes.[39] The law trimmed taxes on dividend income, but did not reduce taxes on withdrawals from annuities, as many insurers had hoped it would. Many advisors argued that lower capital gains rates and lower taxes on dividends would make taxable investments more appealing than annuities. Instead, the growth of the annuity market continued, with increased interest in fixed and indexed annuities.

Tax laws change. That's what legislators do. Insurance companies respond with improved product offerings. Investors seize new opportunities. That's what we all do. We adapt.

Is An Annuity Right For You?

When faced with uncertain economic conditions, people begin to assess the safety of their retirement nest egg. Concern about the return *of* principal can suddenly seem more pressing than the return *on* principal. Wanting to ensure that a portion of your portfolio is insulated from the volatile markets inevitably puts annuities on the plate of options. Annuities aren't for everyone, however. Following are a few indicators that you might be a good candidate:

You Want to Balance Your Portfolio

Any investment should be considered in light of a holistic financial portrait. You will want to assess the strength of your portfolio against the backdrop of your current financial situation, goals, priorities, and tolerance for risk. Look for a mix that offers *your* appropriate blend of growth and safety, risk and reward, liquidity and commitment.

An annuity can provide balance and stability to any portfolio. You can build a portfolio around a base of annuities, or use an annuity to supplement to an established portfolio. This is a matter of taste and situational considerations.

The Time is Right

Deferred annuities are long term commitments generally used for retirement savings. Therefore, the best time to purchase an annuity is when you have satisfied your most critical planning requirements and can afford the long term commitment. You need enough time to allow for significant accumulation. In general, ten years or more provide sufficient time to accumulate growth and optimize tax deferral.

You might want to consider a *laddered strategy* – purchasing a series of deferred annuities starting 10 to 15 years prior to retirement. Not only does this allow you to accumulate growth over varying intervals of time, it allows you to activate income at different stages in the future, thereby optimizing payouts and tax deferral. The later you activate your lifetime income, the greater the income payout. So this strategy can offset the higher costs of inflation.

If you don't have time on your side, an immediate annuity can also stabilize a post-retirement portfolio. Some investors choose the income stability offered by a SPIA, while they continue to play the market with other parts of their retirement portfolios. Again, this is a matter of risk tolerance.

You Have Lost Your Taste for Risk

There are many reasons why people develop a low tolerance for risk. Some inherited a low risk tolerance from their parents. Others bear the scars of past investment catastrophes, and have decided that the often empty promises of stock market returns were not worth the sleepless nights. Still others simply lose their taste for risk the closer they get to retirement – when they can see that their opportunities to replace losses will soon dwindle. Whatever the reasons, if you find yourself wringing your hands over risk and uncertainty, an annuity might be the right thing for you.

8

What Is Your Number?

"When it is obvious that the goals cannot be reached, don't adjust the goals, adjust the action steps." Confucius

Before you get to the stage of evaluating whether annuities are a fit for you, you will probably have a much more fundamental question: How much will you need to retire? Ask ten experts to give you a number off the cuff, you will likely hear a range as wide as Texas.

For years, conventional wisdom has pointed to a nest egg of **$1.0-1.5 million** in order to retire comfortably. In a survey of affluent investors in 2015, Legg Mason found that investors were targeting **$2.5 million** for retirement.[40] Fidelity Investments, one of the nation's largest providers of retirement accounts, suggests saving **at least eight times your ending salary by retirement**.[41] Other experts say that your savings should amount to **10 to 12 times** your current income.[42] Or perhaps you have heard that you need to replace **80 percent of your current income** in retirement.[43] Regardless of which approach you favor, generic benchmarks vary widely.

For people approaching retirement, these kinds of figures can sound alarming, daunting, or even overblown. In reality, there is no magic number. How much *you* need for retirement will differ from the guy next door, because *your* desires, spending habits, obligations, health and life expectancy are unique to you. There simply is no quick, easy or standard answer to the question of how much you will need.

Nevertheless, you need a plan. To have enough money to support your life when you are no longer working, you have to have a saving target. Luckily, the financial community can offer some tips to support your planning process – ranging from top-down income-driven methodologies to bottom-up expense forecasts.

Income Replacement Rate

Income replacement rate is one of the most common guidelines advisors use to estimate how much a client will need in retirement. When Employee Benefits Research Institute[44] asked workers what percentage of their pre-retirement income they thought they would need to live comfortably in retirement, most workers (56%) concluded that they could manage with 70 percent of their pre-retirement income or less. Another 23 percent expected it would take **70– 85 percent of pre-retirement income**. While 16 percent of workers said it would take at least 85 percent. Interestingly, these ratios appear to be in line with actual experiences reported by retirees.

An 80 percent replacement rate means that a worker earning $100,000 per year before retirement needs to save enough to produce an annual income of $80,000 adjusted for inflation during retirement.

While this is an interesting number, it's a bit theoretical until you convert it into a targeted nest egg with an actual savings plan to achieve it. So, how do you do that? This chapter presents a few options.

Generic Saving Rate

If you're in your mid-thirties and looking for an easy rule of thumb, use the saving rate suggested by Boston College's Center for Retirement Research in their 2011 brief, *How Much to Save for a Secure Retirement*.[45] The study showed that an average earner who starts saving at age 35 and retires at 67 needs to save 18 percent each year to build a nest egg sufficient to produce 80% replacement income (assuming a 4-percent return). Naturally, a more precise saving rate depends on earnings, start age, retirement age, returns, and other sources of cash; however, saving 18 percent of your earnings per year is a generally safe bet. And start early! When it comes to saving for retirement, it turns out that starting early and working longer are even more powerful than earning higher returns.

Online Calculators

Another way you can covert the 80% replacement target into a savings plan is to use an online calculator. A quick internet search for "retirement account calculator" will yield several options. Bankrate.com offers a nice one.[46] It prompts you to enter assumptions about age, income, savings, lifespan, and inflation, and uses this information to estimate replacement income, portfolio values, and how long your money will last. For example, a 35 year old currently earning $100,000, expecting income growth of 2% annually, with plans to save 18% of her income per year from a starting point of zero, will have a portfolio worth $1.4 million at 65, assuming a 5% return. The calculator computes her last year's income ($177,500) and uses that to estimate her desired 80% replacement income of $142,000. Then it estimates that she will exhaust her retirement funds at age 76 if she withdraws at that rate (unless, of course, she invests in an annuity with an income rider which will provide income for life). The Bankrate calculator even allows you to add estimated Social Security. If our example investor adds social security to the scenario, her funds will last until age 83. The calculator is organized to allow you to play around with the assumptions until you come up with a scenario that you can live with.

Some experts argue that an 80% replacement target could be overblown. In *Estimating the True Cost of Retirement*,[47] David Blanchett of Morningstar Investment Management group used government data and Monte Carlo simulations to test the 80 percent guideline. While he found a replacement rate between 70% and 80% to be **a reasonable starting place** for most households, actual spending patterns showed that many retirees can get by with about 20% less than that. Before you jump up and down with glee, remember that needs vary. Scrutinize your own spending patterns, add some potential unexpected hits like health insurance or caring for elderly parents, and do your own math. Think of the 80% income replacement rate as a stake in the ground. It's a helpful benchmark when you're beginning to plan. The closer you get to retirement, the more rigorous you can be with your own budget. You may find that your lifestyle and needs require less (or more) than 80% replacement income.

Professional Advice

Ask your advisor to help you develop a plan to bridge the gap between what you have today and what you'll need in the future. In the end, your number is unique. An advisor can tease out requirements you might not have considered. Do you have dependents – perhaps an elderly parent or special needs child? Is leaving an inheritance important to you? How might life insurance fit into your equation? Do you have sources of income you may not have considered? How is your health? Do you have a plan for long term care? There are a host of considerations that may not occur to you when you're thinking of today's spending patterns.

You may want some support when you're sifting through the options, looking for financial products with features and value suitable for your requirements. There are a lot of alternatives – each presenting their own set of pros and cons. A little expert help can go a long way when surfing the sea of possibilities.

The 4 Percent Rule

The "4 percent rule" is a retirement planning strategy introduced by financial planner Bill Bengen in the early 90's. In a nutshell, the theory posits that you will need enough savings when you retire to be able to live on a **4% withdrawal in your first year of retirement**. After the first year, you can **adjust for inflation** each year for **30 years of retirement** without bearing a significant risk of running out of money. Naturally, this rule applies to non-guaranteed accounts. Annuities provide payout structures that satisfy the same goal.

For example, if you withdrew 4% from your $1 million dollar nest egg in your first year of retirement, you would have $40,000 to live on (plus whatever income you might have from other sources such as social security). As long as your expenses stay below that number – assuming that inflation and market returns remain in check – you can be relatively confident that your savings will last for 30 years (without a guarantee).

The "rule" is really more of a "guideline," because no formula is infallible. Like all strategies, Bengen's 4% withdrawal theory is based on some assumptions. It assumes an evenly split portfolio of stocks and bonds whose performance mimics historical market conditions. While a weak market of historic proportions could certainly obviate the 4% rule, the theory has stood the test of time and weathered a fair bit of scrutiny. So, it's a reasonable place *to start*.

You can use the 4% withdrawal guideline to calculate your targeted retirement nest egg. Simply divide your projected annual spending in retirement by four percent. Or, reverse the math, and multiply your projected annual spending by 25.

- **Targeted Savings** = Projected annual retirement spending / 0.04
- **Targeted Savings** = Projected annual retirement spending x 25

If you have no idea what your spending will be, use the 80% replacement rate described earlier to come up with an estimate. For instance, if you currently earn $50,000, your projected annual retirement spending target will be $40,000 per year (including taxes). In this case, you will need to save $1,000,000. (i.e., $40,000 / 0.04 or $40,000 x 25). On the other hand, if you expect to spend $100,000 annually, the 4% rule says that you will need a cool $2.5 million (i.e., $100,000 x 25) to support your lifestyle and needs.

If you are already nearing retirement, you can test your savings level with the same 4% guideline. For instance, $500,000 in savings will point to a $20,000 first-year withdrawal (i.e., $500,000 x 0.04), adjusted for inflation in the years after that.

Estimated annual retirement income = Total savings x 4%

Only you can decide whether the resulting number is sufficient or insufficient and what to do about it. Your income, interests, and life can be influenced by so many uncontrollable factors that no formula could possibly work 100 percent of the time. If a 4% withdrawal rate seems too high, assume a different percentage and adjust the calculation accordingly. Remember that other sources of income (e.g., pensions, social security, real estate, inheritance, etc.) can substantially reduce the amount you'll need from your investments. On the other hand, if the computed dollar amount seems too low to support your needs – and you don't have other sources of income or the time to earn it – you may need to scrutinize your expenses. Don't make the mistake of over-spending in your early retirement years, increasing the risk that you will outlive your savings. When there is no more money coming in, you have to be extra vigilant to protect what you have.

Not everyone is a fan of the 4% rule. Many advisors argue that the 4% rule fails to account for investment costs, variable spending, and tax brackets. An investor who pays a financial advisor 2% of assets annually, for example, might find the 4% rule to be impractical.

Other critics point out that the 4 percent rule was created during a specific time in economic history that may not be replicated. Interest rates were so low and stock markets so high in recent history that it's hard to know whether these conditions will hold long enough for the 4 percent rule to work for future retirees.

Whether the future is molded by a worst- or best-case scenario remains to be seen. We will know when we know. In the meantime, the 4 percent rule is better than nothing for estimating purposes. How much you *actually* need to retire is a number that only you can decide based on your lifestyle considerations, health, financial obligations, interests and income sources.

Whether you buy into the 4% rule or not, your best bet is to start saving now and to save a lot. As the old proverb goes, "a penny saved is a penny earned." There is no time when this wisdom rings more true than in your retirement years.

Planning From the Bottom Up

Both replacement income and the 4% rule focus on the top line: How much income will you want in retirement? It's a reasonable approach if you are early in the planning process and have no way of estimating future expenses. As you near retirement age, however, income is probably not as important as expenses when thinking about your nest egg.

Conventional wisdom says that you want to accumulate enough savings to cover *25 years* of expenses in retirement. That's a reasonable time horizon for the *average* person nearing retirement in this day and age. According to the U.S. Social Security Administration, the average 65 year old man is expected to live until 84, and the average 65-year-old woman is projected to live to

87. Lifespan statistics also show, however, that if current life expectancy trends continue, more than half of babies born in wealthy nations today will live to 100 years. While averages are useful benchmarks, remember that you might be the lucky one who is better than average. So, it pays to have the kind of back-up plan an annuity can offer in the event that you knock the averages out of the park!

The closer you are to retirement, the less satisfied you should be with rules of thumb to determine your number. At some point, you simply have to put a pen to paper and figure out how much you are likely to spend. You can develop a realistic plan – tailored to your particular needs – in five easy steps.

1. **Expenses:** Tally up your anticipated expenses as a proxy for determining how much income you will need. This chapter will provide some tips on where you may spend less (or more) than you were used to spending during your prime earning years.

2. **Income Requirements:** Determine the income you expect to receive from sources other than savings (e.g., Social Security, pension, rental income, etc.), then figure out the gap between that number and your expected expenses. This is the gap you will need to close with savings.

3. **Gap Closure:** Develop a plan to close the gap between what you have today and what you'll need for retirement.

4. **Time Horizon:** Estimate how long you expect to be retired. Most of the planning rules of thumb assume 25-30 years. If you think that will meet your requirements, then carry on.

If you're not sure, you may want to plan to save more and/or consider using annuities to provide a safety net.

5. **Your Safe Money:** Determine what percentage of your portfolio will be dedicated to "safe" money. Annuities can be a good fit for this part of your portfolio.

Food for Thought

The good news is that most people can live on far less than their peak earnings once their children are independent and their home is paid off. According to the Consumer Expenditure Survey (CES) produced by the U.S. Bureau of Labor Statistics[48], household spending peaks between ages 35 to 54, then continues to decline with age.

Figure 22

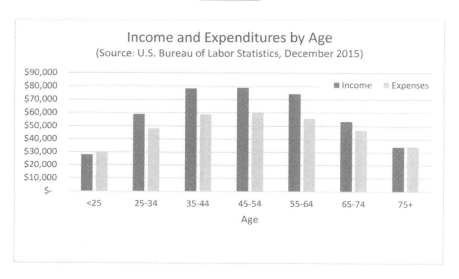

The average consumer aged 65 and older spent less in almost every spending category:

- 61-89% less on Social Security and pension-related savings
- 52% less on transportation
- 38-61% less on clothing and related services
- 48% less on food
- 24-40% less on housing-related costs
- 14-54% less on entertainment

Judging from these indicators, you may find that you can live comfortably on 40-50% less than your pre-retirement income. It makes sense. As kids grow up and move away, family-related costs go down. Anyone who has paid for dance classes, sports, braces, childcare, and college knows that kids consume a chunk of change. Babycenter.com estimates that it takes a mid-income family $12,000-14,000 per year to raise a child. It's no surprise then that smaller households would spend less on most goods and services when compared to larger households. Similarly, you would expect work-related expenditures – like clothing, transportation, 401k contributions, and Social Security – to go down after retirement. After all, a life of leisure doesn't demand business suits, car pools, or parking fees. And since retirees are more likely to be consuming Social Security benefits and savings than to be making contributions, you can subtract that from your historical monthly outflow.

The only *exception* to the rule of expense windfalls CES found with age was healthcare. As you might expect, out-of-pocket healthcare expenses go up with age – both in dollar amount and as a share of total household budget. Survey results revealed that the average 65-74 year old consumer in 2013 spent $5,188 out of pocket per year on healthcare – more than 5.5 times what they spent in their youth – consuming as much as 14.3 percent of household income in their later years.

These data points are meant to provide food for thought as you put together your post-retirement expense plan. Clearly, there is evidence that retiree's spending habits change during retirement and that consumer spending goes down with age. What is not so clear, however, is whether the reduction is voluntary or forced as financial resources dwindle.

Nevertheless, if you are open to the idea that your consumption habits will change, you might need less than many analysts predict. There is a gigantic difference between planning to live in the lap of luxury versus planning for the income needed to honestly meet your retirement needs. It's up to you to decide where you fall in this rather wide range of possibilities.

Tally Your Expenses

With these statistics as a backdrop, put some thought to your own number. Start by figuring out approximately how much you'll need to spend in retirement on an annual basis. If you use a financial software package like Quicken, you can simply print out your annual expenses as a starting point. If you don't have a detailed history, you can back into it using your current earnings. With a few important adjustments, your earnings can be recast to provide a baseline expense budget. Simply deduct the following expenses from your current baseline:

- **Deduct the amount you currently save:** Obviously, after you retire, you won't need to save for retirement anymore.

- **Deduct payroll tax:** Since you won't have a paycheck anymore, you won't have payroll tax.
- **Reduce income tax:** Some of your money may come from tax qualified accounts (e.g., 401k, SEP), so you will still pay income taxes. But, it will probably be less than what you're paying now.
- **Reduce housing expenses:** If you expect to pay off your mortgage, you can deduct that amount. If you plan on downsizing or moving to a lower cost region, deduct anticipated savings in taxes, utilities, insurance, maintenance and other household expenses.
- **Reduce work-related expenses.** When you are no longer working, the cost of commuting, parking, lunches out, and clothing go down.
- **Factor in expenses related to your children.** As your kids leave the nest and become independent, you will generally spend less in this category.

You may also need to add a few budget items:

- **Factor in expected lifestyle changes.** If you intend to travel the world or buy a yacht in retirement, vacation expenses might actually increase for a while.
- **Plan for higher healthcare costs.** If you have been paying for your own individual health insurance, your medical insurance might even go down when you join Medicare. If your employer has covered your insurance for years, you might be shocked to find how much this can cost. Most people will spend more on health-related services as they age. The best plan is to investigate health insurance options and to assess your own health as realistically as you can.

Your annual expense requirements are mostly driven by your own choices. You have a lot of control over how you're going to live your life in retirement. If you are willing to make a few concessions, these adjustments can reduce your cost of living by as much as forty or fifty percent. Throttling back on post-retirement expenses slightly ultimately means that you can save less before retirement (or retire earlier).

"I deem myself a wealthy man because my income exceeds my expenses and my expenses equal my desires." Edward Gibbon

Tally Your Income

During the working years, most people depend on one source of income – a job. In retirement, however, your annual income will likely stream from several sources. It's important to understand how your potential retirement income streams stack up. The most common sources include:

- Retirement accounts (e.g., 401k, IRA, Keogh, SEP)
- Social Security
- Stocks
- Savings (e.g., certificates of deposit and bank accounts)
- Pensions
- Rent and royalties
- Inheritance
- Annuities or insurance
- Part-time work
- Home equity

Using the list above, add up the value of the assets you expect to tap for retirement income and multiply that number by 4%. As you may recall, this formula will give you an idea of what you could expect to safely withdraw each year with inflation adjustments to fund a 30-year retirement. Remember, this is a rule of thumb, not a guarantee. If you want a guarantee – buy an annuity!

Is it enough? To answer this question, subtract your annual expense estimate from your annual income estimate.

Saving surplus (or deficit) = Estimated income - estimated expenses

If the result is a positive number (i.e., more income than expenses) or break-even, you probably have enough income to support your retirement needs. High-five! However, if the result is negative, it means you have a deficit (i.e., expenses greater than income). For example, if you think your annual expenses will be $50,000 versus $40,000 in income, then you have a $10,000 deficit per year that you will have to address. There are three ways to deal with a deficit: (1) save more to bridge the gap, (2) throttle back on expenses so that you don't spend more than you have, or (3) do some of each.

Another way to check your retirement readiness is to multiple your estimated annual expenses by 25. If that number matches (or is less than) your total income sources, then you are retirement-ready. For example, if your expected annual expenses are $50,000 and you have $1.25 million (i.e., 50,000 x 25) or more in your total income source pool, then you're golden. If you have less than that, you'll need to save more or spend less.

Bridge the Gap

In order to bridge the gap between what you need and what you have, you will want to convert the deficit into a savings plan. Simply multiply your annual deficit by 25. That gives you the amount you need to save in order to withdraw the recommended 4 percent annually.

For example, suppose you anticipate spending $50,000 per year to keep yourself housed, clothed, nourished, and happy in retirement. You have a pension that will provide $20,000 per year, Social Security will pay $18,000, and if you withdraw 4% from your $200,000 CD each year you can add another $8,000 to the annual income stream. That's a total of $46,000 in income per year – resulting in a shortfall of $4,000 per year versus expenses. In order to bridge that gap, you will need to save another $100,000 (i.e., 4,000 x 25) before retirement in order to support that kind of spending level during retirement.

Time Horizon

An important element of retirement planning is estimating how long you expect to be retired. To put it morbidly, your time horizon is the difference between the age you expect to retire and the age you expect to expire. Since there's no crystal ball to accurately predict your lifespan, this part takes a solid dose of personal guesswork.

Social Security Administration statistics say that the average 65 year old today will live about 20 more years. But, remember, these are statistics for the masses. They work for insurance companies who can play the odds, but it's not helpful on a personal level. All it tells you is that you have about a 50/50 chance of living longer. You have to apply some of your own wisdom to "guesstimate" your time horizon. Myabaris.com offers a life expectancy calculator that uses information about your health, education, financial status, and other indicators to give you a personal life expectancy estimate. That's slightly better than mass statistics.

Obviously, time matters. If you live to 105 and want to spend your last 25 years in an expensive retirement community, you will need a bigger chunk of change than if you are hit by a bus at age 68. The problem is, you don't know. And simply accepting the risk that you could run out of savings before you run out of life seems to be an unacceptable risk. That's where insurance comes in. It's the whole premise of this book. Annuities provide a safety net to address that unknown. They are the only financial vehicle available today that insure your future income for *life* – no matter how long that might be.

Have a Safe Money Target

Advice about creating a balanced portfolio can be found on every corner – and frequently aggressive strategies built on volatile, *potentially* lucrative, stock markets get the lion's share of attention. While I am the first to admit that there is no one-size-fits-all portfolio strategy, I am shocked at how often I meet with retirees whose portfolios are heavily invested in volatile and risky investments. By now you have seen how detrimental a decline in portfolio value can be in the distribution stage of your financial journey. Dedicating an important part of your portfolio to **safe money** becomes more and more essential as you approach retirement.

There is no correct asset allocation by age – that will depend on your personal situation and risk tolerance. However, it never hurts to start with a rule of thumb to kick start the conversation. A common guidepost is to subtract your age from 100 to get the percentage of your portfolio which could be invested in stocks. For example, if you're 30, you could keep 70% of your portfolio in stocks without too much concern. If you're 70 on the other hand, a better bet is 30% in stocks – reserving 70% for safe money. The general premise is that your risk tolerance should go down as you age, because you will be less likely to generate replacement income and have less time to recover from a portfolio loss.

Take a hard look at your portfolio and honestly assess where your investments stand on the risk continuum – rank them on a scale from 1 to 10. Does your portfolio mix reflect your current personal risk tolerance and stage of life – or is it a remnant of decisions past? Which of your investments are exposed to market volatility? If your portfolio dropped 50% in one year, could you easily recover? Where is your safe money? What percent of your retirement nest egg do you want to keep safe? How will your current portfolio meet your objective of creating sustainable income for life?

Every retiree has his or her own idea of safety. Some people want the certainty and peace of mind that come with a lifelong income stream. Others want predictable growth with the flexibility to withdraw money as needs arise. Leaving a legacy for heirs might be of critical importance to one person, while the next guy is focused on keeping up with inflation. No matter what your retirement expectations are, annuities often out-perform other safe money options while offering guarantees that can sustain your future income.

Start Here

If your goal is a lifetime of income – and the peace of mind that comes with it – start now.

1. Determine your number and quantify your gap.
2. Assess your portfolio versus your income goal, risk tolerance, personal circumstances, and assumptions. Set a target for safe money.
3. List your priorities (e.g., lifetime income, dependents, death benefits, liquidity, risk-reward, etc.)
4. Meet with an annuity expert to evaluate the options and select the option that is best for you.

And so the journey begins. May your retirement be joyful and carefree, with income sufficient to support your needs and whims … for life!

Supplement: Just for Fun!

Planning how you will invest retirement years for maximum enjoyment and development is as important as planning for the income to support it. Want some inspiration? Here you will find some of the activities retirees look forward to most, along with a few resources to support your journey.

Travel. When you're working and raising your family, you have to work around school years, and shoehorn travel into limited vacation days. In retirement, however, time limitations disappear. You'll have more freedom to travel during off-peak times of the year which tend to be more affordable. Plus, you can stay as long as you want to. Go live in a foreign country for a while or take a long cruise. If you are interested in combining wanderlust with learning, check out Road Scholar (www.**roadscholar**.org) — an organization dedicated to educational travel offering 6,500 educational tours in all 50 states and 150 countries.

Spend more time with friends and family. One popular retirement ambition is to be with loved ones. Give this idea some wings by listing creative ways to share time. Chances are, you have some remarkable places within a two hour drive, or even within walking distance, of where you live. Look at "Things to Do" on FamilyNow.com to prime the old idea pump.

Improve your home. Retirees can finally pursue those long-delayed projects to jazz up their homes. It could be something simple like organizing your stuff or something big like adding space. You'll have the time, so learn to make the changes yourself.

Get some exercise and beautify your home by taking up gardening. Grow organic vegetables and feed your interest in healthy cooking. Not sure how to get started? YouTube provides oodles of free how-to videos on nearly any topic you can dream up.

Keep working. According to CareerBuilder's 2015 retirement survey[49], 54% of workers over the age of 60 intend to work after retiring from their current career — up from 45% the prior year. Of this group, 81% expect to work part-time citing customer service, retail and consulting as desirable choices for their retirement career. I know one couple who combines learning, travel and work by pursuing unique jobs in areas they want to explore. For example, they moved to Napa Valley and worked at a winery for a year. They learned about wine, made a few extra bucks, explored a new region and met a completely new set of friends. A well planned retirement allows you to pursue working interests without being overly influenced by compensation. You can work simply for the joy of working, so get creative.

Learn something new. Retirement is the perfect time to learn something new — and universities frequently offer seniors low-cost opportunities to feed the mind. Ask your local college if they offer senior citizen tuition waivers or allow retirees to audit classes which haven't been filled with paying students. If you are more of a home body, try online courses from the comfort of your living room. All you need is a personal computer and Internet connection! Coursera (www.**coursera**.org) and edX (www.**edx.org)** both offer free online courses taught by professors at major universities.

Learn to play the piano, guitar, or your favorite instrument. According to Suzanne Hanser, chair of the music therapy department at the Berklee College of Music in Boston, music-making is linked to a number of health benefits for older adults[50]. Learning includes hobbies. Take on something new such as painting, photography, fishing, sculpture, hiking, chess, woodworking or gardening. Even something simple like playing a new card game can activate the old brain cells.

Exercise. Once you retire, you will no longer be able to claim that you are too busy to exercise. Join a gym. Hike. Bike. Kayak. Swim. Walk your dog. Go on a llama trek. Climb a mountain. Go white water rafting. Learn to dance. Try yoga or Tai Chi. Take a self-defense class. Jog. Ski. Box. Play tennis, racquetball or squash. Take up gardening. Join a kick-boxing, stair stepping, cycling, weight-lifting, or cross-fit class. If competition is your thing, participate in the National Senior Games (nsga.com). Hire a trainer, recruit some fellow athletes, or go it alone. Just do it. Move. Having a strong and healthy body will make your retirement years so much more enjoyable.

Experience another culture. When you're no longer tied to a job, you can live anywhere in the world. Some retirees plan to spend their retirement years living abroad. Need some ideas? International Living (http://internationalliving.com) annually combines real-world insights about climate, health care, cost of living, and other interesting tidbits to provide a comprehensive list of the best bang-for-your buck retirement destinations on the planet.

If you're worried about leaving family and friends in the U.S. for extended periods of time, arrange mini-retirements and live abroad for 6 months. If traveling isn't in the cards, you can still challenge yourself by learning a foreign language and practicing with a native speaker.

Read and Write. Read all of the books you never had time to read. Pick a topic you want to master, savor your way through the classics or dive into biographies of your favorite historical figures. Add a social element to your passion by joining (or starting) a book club. If you like to write, chances are there's a book inside of you. Writing a book takes time and, as a retiree, you'll have plenty of it. So, write your novel, a cookbook, a how-to guide, or your memoirs.

Learn to blog, and share your experience online like Sydney Lagier, who blogs at *Retirement: A Full-Time Job*. Select a topic you have already mastered or blog about your journey as you explore a new interest. Write in your journal. Write to friends. Just write.

Volunteer. There is no shortage of volunteer opportunities available for retirees if you are willing to donate your time and efforts. Look for volunteer positions that match the interests and skills honed during your working life. Re-purpose your project management skills or carpentry interests to work with Habitat for Humanity. Put your legal prowess to work by advocating for foster children.

Want to learn while you volunteer? Universities and museums have docent programs. Need a furry fix? Work at an animal shelter or consider serving as a "foster parent" until a permanent home can be found for a homeless dog or cat. Want to stop hunger? Look into Meals on Wheels. Help the troops? Try USO or Veterans Affairs Volunteer Services (VAVS). Interested in politics? Volunteer for a political campaign, grassroots organization, or political action committee.

Your prospects are endless. **Simply have fun!**

About the Authors
Debbie Andrews

Since launching her financial planning career, Debbie Andrews has been helping clients improve their long term financial success. She is passionate about helping clients make sound and educated decisions suited to their unique situations.

Debbie founded Andrews Financial Services in 1989 and is Security Licensed in Series 7, Series 63, Series 65, and Group 1 Life & Health Insurance – qualifying her to support clients across a wide range of financial strategies from insurance and annuities to market-related portfolios.

Andrews Financial Services provides services related to retirement planning, estate tax planning, investing and other life financial goals. With a keen interest in long-term planning, Debbie has developed a deep expertise in principal protected options, annuities and life insurance, IRA's, SEP's, 401(k) investments, mutual funds, and long term care. She particularly enjoys educating her clients, identifying personalized solutions, and building lasting relationships.

Debbie is a native Texan, has two sons, and lives in Houston, Texas with her husband of 36 years.

Kathryn Payne

As President of Reach Enterprises, Kathryn enjoyed 28 years as a management consultant – working with leaders of international corporations to produce business results by engaging people. With a knack for communications and change management, she earned a reputation for being able to translate complex strategies into simple language and stepwise action.

As co-author of this book, Kathryn offers these skills to the reader by representing the voice of an investor. She focuses on addressing common questions and ensuring direct answers while keeping financial jargon in check. Because she is an independent investor interested in answering these questions for herself, Kathryn works well with Debbie Andrews to distill annuities to their essence using layman's terms.

Resources

Following are a few resources you might find to be helpful for financial planning.

- http://www.andrewsfinancial.net/ provides a host of articles and reference documents on investing, retirement, estate planning, tax planning, cash management, and risk management.
- http://www.usinflationcalculator.com/ provides historical inflation rates from 1914 to 2016. Rates of inflation are calculated using the current Consumer Price Index published monthly by the Bureau of Labor Statistics (BLS).
- http://moneychimp.com/ offers a plethora of tools including calculators (e.g., retirement planning, savings, IRA, tax, payroll tax, capital gains, market CAGR, inflation, etc.), explanations of common financial formulas (e.g., compound interest, bond yields, CAGR, etc.), and instructions for reading annual reports.
- www.nolhga.com This site provides industry facts, figures, and other useful information regarding annuities and life insurance.
- http://www.bankrate.com offers several nice tools, including a retirement account calculator to help you estimate your nest egg. It also offers CD rates and other comparative information.
- https://www.myabaris.com/ provides a longevity calculator. Enter a few facts about yourself and it will calculate your estimated life span.
- http://www.bls.gov/bls/proghome.htm : The Bureau of Labor Statistics offers a wealth of information about the economy and the workers who fuel it.
- www.PersonalCapital.com allows you to aggregate and track all of your investments in one place.
- www.PersonalFunds.com provides a cost calculator for comparing the cost of various funds.
- www.marketwatch.com offers current and historical market data from around the world

References

[1] Jennie L. Phipps, *20 Things We Do in Retirement*, Bankrate.com, December 3, 2014

[2] Charlene M. Kalenkoski and Eakamon Oumtrakool, *How Retirees Spend Their Time: Helping Clients Set Realistic Income Goals*, Journal of Financial Planning, 2014

[3] Jacquelyn B. James, Elyssa Besen, Christina Matz-Costa, and Marcie Pitt-Catsouphes, *Insights on Activity in Later Life from the Life & Times in an Aging Society Study—Engaged as We Age*, Sloan Center on Aging and Work at Boston College, January 2012

[4] http://www.catholiccharities.org/pages/content-migration/mamie-george-community-center

[5] Jack Marrion, *A Little Annuity History*, Advantage Compedium, March 2010

[6] John Suchet, *Beethoven's history 1803-1812*, http://www.classicfm.com

[7] Pensions & Investments, *Steel Baron Andrew Caregie Pioneered Pension Funding*, December 1999, http://www.pionline.com/

[8] *Benjamin Franklin's Bequest*, https://en.wikipedia.org/wiki/Benjamin_Franklin#Bequest

[9] *The Babe, The Great Depression, and Annuities*, Annuity Reserve, April 27, 2012

[10] Damian Davila, *Ben Bernanke's financial advice: Money isn't everything*, The Christian Science Monitor, June 11, 2015

[11] *What OJ Simpson Can Teach Us About Domestic Asset Protection*, http://www.Mwpatton.com, Jan 14th, 2013

[12] *Treasury Issues Guidance to Encourage Annuities in 401(k) Plans*, U.S. Department of the Treasury Press Center, October 24, 2014

[13] *Ensuring Income throughout Retirement Requires Difficult Choices*, GAO Report to the Chairman, Special Committee on Aging, U.S. Senate, June 2011

[14] Honor Whiteman, *Life Expectancy in the US Reaches Record High*, Medical News Today, October 8, 2014, http://www.medicalnewstoday.com/articles/283625.php

[15] Stephanie Brunner, *Current Life Expectancy Trends And Challenges: Will We Live To Be 100 Years?*, Medical News Today, October 2, 2009, http://www.medicalnewstoday.com/articles/165960.php

[16] *Global Health and Aging*, National Institute on Aging, Health & Aging, Updated January 22, 2015, https://www.nia.nih.gov/research/publication/global-health-and-aging/living-longer

[17] *Global Health and Aging*, National Institute on Aging, Health & Aging, Updated January 22, 2015, https://www.nia.nih.gov/research/publication/global-health-and-aging/living-

longer

[18] U.S. Bureau of the Census (1999), http://www.census.gov/

[19] *American Family Financial* Statistics, Statistic Brain Research Institute, August 12, 2015

20 http://www.moneychimp.com/features/market_cagr.htm

21 Mark P. Cussen, Is Annuitization Your Best Strategy?, Investopedia

22 Aaron Neishlos, What Does It Mean *to Annuitize a Variable Annuity,* http://www.annuityfyi.com

[23] Marc Davis, *Top 6 U.S. Government Financial Bailouts,* October 13, 2008; http://www.investopedia.com

[24] www.nolhga.com

[25] Shelly K. Schwartz, *How secure is life insurance?,* Bankrate.com

[26] *The Nation's Safety Net, 2014 Edition,* www.nolhga.com,

[27] *Quantitative Analysis Of Investor Behavior,* Dalbar, 2012

[28] Lance Roberts, *Why You Can't Beat the Index,* Street Talk Live, April 2, 2013

[29] *Compound Annual Growth Rate (Annualized Return),* MoneyChimp.com,

[30] *Worst Stock Market Crashes,* March 2011 http://www.worststockmarketcrashes.com/stock-market-crashes/wall-streets-worst-market-crashes/

[31] *Japanese asset price bubble,* Wikipedia.com

[32] *Overview of BLS Statistics on Inflation and Prices,* Bureau of Labor Statistics, http://www.bls.gov/bls/inflation.htm

[33] Sumit Agarwal, John C. Driscoll, Xavier Gabaix, and David Laibson, *The Age of Reason: Financial Decisions over the Life-Cycle with Implications for Regulation,* https://dash.harvard.edu, October 19, 2009

[34] Jeffery Brown, *Use Annuities to Protect Yourself from Yourself,* Forbes, May 22, 2014

[35] Michael Maye, *Average Investor 20 Year Return Astoundingly Awful,* July 18,2012, http://www.thestreet.com

[36] Ty A. Bernicke, *The Real Cost of Owning a Mutual Fund,* Forbes, April 4, 2011

[37] *Average Financial Advisor Fees in 2016,* Advisoryhq.com,. February 16, 2016

[38] Hazel Bradford, *Business Insurance, DOL moving forward on retirement investment advice fiduciary rule,* August 17, 2015, http://www.businessinsurance.com

[39] Matthew Lubanko, *Tax Cuts Threaten Variable Annuity Sales,* Hartford Courant, June 14, 2003

[40] Legg Mason, *U.S. Investors Need $2.5 Million for Retirement,* Mar 9, 2015 www.leggmason.com/press/releases/03_09_2015.pdf,

[41] *Fidelity: Put Aside 8 Times Your Salary Before You Retire,* Cnbc.com, Friday, 14 Sep 2012

[42] *You'll Need 11 Times Your Salary for Retirement,* Freemoneyfinance.com, July 12, 2012

[43] Christine Benz, *Digging Into the 80% Rule for Income Replacement in Retirement,* Morning Star, November 2013

[44] https://www.ebri.org/surveys/rcs/2015/

[45] Alicia H. Munnell, Anthony Webb, andFrancesca N. Golub-Sass, *How Much to Save for a Secure Retirement,* Boston College, Center for Retirement Research, 2011

[46] http://www.bankrate.com/calculators/index-of-retirement-calculators.aspx

[47] David Blanchett, *Estimating the True Cost of Retirement,* Morningstar Investment Management 22, November 5, 2013

[48] *2014 Consumer Expenditure Survey,* Bureau of Labor Statistics, September 3, 2015, http://www.bls.gov/cex/#tables_long

[49] *Number of senior workers delaying retirement reaches new post-recession low,* Careerbuilder, 2015, http://www.careerbuilder.com

[50] Fred Cicetti, *Is Playing a Musical Instrument Good for Your Health?,* Live Science, October 21, 2013, http://www.livescience.com/40597-playing-musical-instrument-good-health.html

45477193R00091

Made in the USA
San Bernardino, CA
10 February 2017